Vampire Knits

Vampire Knits

PROJECTS TO KEEP YOU KNITTING
FROM TWILIGHT TO DAWN

Genevieve Miller

POTTER
CRAFT

NEW YORK

This book is dedicated to knitters and vampire lovers everywhere.

Published in the United States by Potter Craft, an imprint of the
Crown Publishing Group, a division of Random House, Inc., New York.
www.crownpublishing.com
wwww.pottercraft.com

POTTER CRAFT and colophon is a registered trademark of Random House, Inc.

Library of Congress Cataloging-in-Publication Data

Miller, Genevieve, 1969-
 Vampire knits : projects to keep you knitting from twilight to dawn / by
Genevieve Miller. -- 1st ed.
    p. cm.
  Includes index.
  ISBN-13: 978-0-307-58660-5 [alk. paper]
  ISBN-10: 0-307-58660-X [alk. paper]
  1. Knitting--Patterns. I. Title.
  TT825.M564 2010
  746.43'2--DC22

                    2010014869

Printed in the United States

Design by Laura Palese
Photography by Heather Weston
Author photograph by Candice Eley
Photograph from Forks, Washington, page 130 by Tere Mendez
Illustrations by Kara Gott Warner

10 9 8 7 6 5 4 3 2 1

First Edition

Acknowledgments

Special thanks to my family and friends for their support, especially my husband Wayne and my children Sean, Grace, and Madeline, who've been infinitely patient and supportive of this project. I love you all! Thanks to Ravelry, where the idea for this book was born, for introducing me to the great fans of TWILIGHT and other vampire stories. Thanks to all the women of the tkb and the Vampire Knits group who gave their time, talents, and efforts to design, offer ideas and feedback, and test knit the projects. Thanks to all the writers and moviemakers who've given us such rich characters to draw from. Thanks to Amy Polcyn, our technical editor, who standardized patterns from several designers and to Matt Terich for making all the charts uniform. Special thanks to Tere Mendez for making the long trek to Forks, Washington and the Hoh Rain Forest to take photos, and to Candice Eley for getting her bat on. A big thanks to Kate Epstein and Betty Wong for believing in our project and helping it along. Thanks to Linda Hetzer, our editor, for making the entire piece cohesive, and Chi Ling Moy for the incredible visual design.

A portion of the proceeds from VAMPIRE KNITS will be donated to The Red Cross, who've been helping humans get the blood they need since before Edward Cullen was born.

SPECIAL THANKS TO THESE YARN COMPANIES WHO PROVIDED YARN FOR THE PROJECTS IN THIS BOOK:

KNITPICKS

PLYMOUTH YARN COMPANY

BERROCO

LOUET

CASCADE YARNS

CONTENTS

INTRODUCTION

I'm a knitter who loves vampires—and I'm not the only one. I started out as your average knitter, making hats, blankets, and sweaters, altering patterns when I couldn't find exactly what I wanted. But it wasn't until I got swept away by Stephenie Meyer's TWILIGHT series that I was inspired to design my own patterns. I've always been intrigued by vampire stories, including those of Anne Rice and even the old Universal Studios Dracula films, but Meyer brought the vampires into the modern day and made them absolutely fascinating. From the first moment Bella laid eyes on her 108-year-old Edward Cullen, I was hooked. I wanted to step inside the books I loved so much and interact with them in my own hands-on way—knitting. My first creation was a scarf that turned me into a willing vampire victim, with "blood" at the neck. When I wear it, people always ask me about it and soon we're discussing the allure of vampires and favorite legends. I've found many people who love the stories as much as I do. (My husband wears the scarf when I let him and often has women stopping him on the street to ask him about it!)

As a member of Ravelry, the online knitting community, it didn't take long for me to find a group of knitters and designers who were similarly enthralled by modern day vampire stories. We fans of mysterious, brooding, and sexy vampires shared ideas and inspiration with one another, creating patterns inspired by beloved immortal characters. And so the idea for this book was born.

Vampires of all kinds are the inspiration for the projects in this book. Perhaps you're a fan of the scary, bloodthirsty vampires of horror films, or the flawlessly beautiful Stefan Salvatore and Edward Cullen, strong otherworldly young men who find love with human girls. Whether you like Joss Whedon's Angel, Spike, and Drusilla; or Charlaine Harris' Southern vampires who like to frequent the same bars we humans do, you'll find a project to make, wear, or give. There are more than 25 projects by vampire fans across the country and beyond. Some of us are knitwear designers, but many of us are students, professionals, or stay-at-home moms who love to knit and design. The patterns are inspired by the vampire characters that have captured our hearts as well as more playful pieces featuring vampire imagery. And because where there are vampires, there are often werewolves, we even have a chapter devoted to our favorite shapeshifters. From knit garments that protect a frail human's most vulnerable areas to items and accessories that any stylish immortal will want, the projects in this book are fun to knit—or, in the case of the jewelry, crochet—and will be one more way to celebrate your vampire obsession.

So grab your stakes—uh, needles—and dig in!

1

PROTECT ME!

It's a dark night, and you're walking home alone. You hear footsteps, and think, "What if it's a vampire?" Well, what if it IS a vampire? How do you protect yourself from the walking un-dead? If you live in Shreveport, Louisiana; Forks, Washington; or a village in the Carpathian Mountains, you could find yourself in the company of vampires. You'll want to be prepared and protected. Even if you like to consort with the Cold Ones, you're going to need some cozy garments to keep you warm and to keep your most tempting veins and arteries under wraps.

In this chapter, you'll find pulse protectors to cover your most vulnerable spots, a head scarf reminiscent of silver bullets, warm mittens and a hooded cowl, a beautiful cover for your diary, and a sweater for your favorite Goth boy.

Pulse Protectors

When a modern girl dates an ancient vampire, it's a good idea to have her pulse points covered. This matching wrist and neck warmer set help give her just enough protection when she's alone with her boyfriend, so he's not as tempted to take a sip.

DESIGNED BY → Kathie Pendry   SKILL LEVEL → Intermediate

SIZE
One size fits most

FINISHED MEASUREMENTS
Wrist warmers: To fit 6" (15cm) wrist
Cowl: Approximately 21" (53cm) in circumference

MATERIALS
Cascade 220 **(4)** medium (100% wool; 3½ oz/100g, 220 yd/200m): 2 skeins in 2422 Lavender → Size 6 (4mm) straight needles → Cable needle → Tapestry needle

GAUGE
20 stitches and 28 rows = 4" (10cm) in stockinette stitch

SPECIAL SKILLS
→ **Cables (page 134)**

SPECIAL INSTRUCTIONS
→ **T3F:** Place 2 stitches on cable needle and hold to front, p1, k2 from cable needle.

→ **T3B:** Place 1 stitch on cable needle and hold to back, k2, p1 from cable needle.

→ **C4F:** Place 2 stitches on cable needle and hold to front, k2, k2 from cable needle.

→ **C4B:** Place 2 stitches on cable needle and hold to back, k2, k2 from cable needle.

NOTE
Stitches between [ ] represent the 18-stitch cable pattern portion of that row.

Left Wrist Warmer
Cast on 34 stitches.
Row 1 (WS): *K2, p2; repeat from * to last 2 stitches, k2.
Row 2: Knit.
Rows 3 and 4: Repeat Rows 1 and 2.
Row 5: P2, M1, p2, M1, (k2, p2) 4 times, k2, p4, M1, p4, M1, p4—38 sts.
Row 6 (RS): K14, [(p2, T3F, T3B) twice, p2], k6.
Row 7 and all WS rows: Knit the knit stitches and purl the purl stitches as they appear.
Row 8: K14, [p3, C4F, p4, C4F, p3], k6.
Row 10: K14, [(p2, T3B, T3F) twice, p2], k6.
Row 12: K14, [p1, (T3B, p2, T3F) twice, p1], k6.
Row 14: K14, [p1, k2, p4, C4B, p4, k2, p1], k6.

· TID-BITE ·

Starting in 1964, we got to watch our friends THE MUNSTERS. While nobody was ever seen drinking blood, Grandpa Munster was the archetypal caricature of a vampire, even driving a car with "Drag-u-la" on the license plate.

Row 16: K14, [p1, (T3F, p2, T3B) twice, p1], k6.

Row 18: Repeat Row 6.

Row 20: Repeat Row 8.

Row 22: Repeat Row 10.

Row 24: Repeat Row 12.

Row 26: Repeat Row 14.

Row 28: Repeat Row 16.

Row 30: K6, k2tog, k6, repeat between [ ] (cable pattern) of Row 6, k6–37 sts.

Row 32: K3, k2tog, k3, k2tog, k3, repeat cable pattern of Row 8, k2, k2tog, k2–34 sts.

Row 34: K11, repeat cable pattern of Row 10, k5.

Row 36: K11, repeat cable pattern of Row 12, k5.

Row 38: K11, repeat cable pattern of Row 14, k5.

Row 40: K4, M1, k3, M1, k4, repeat cable pattern of Row 16, k5–36 sts.

Row 42: K6, M1, k7, repeat cable pattern of Row 6, k2, M1, k3–38 sts.

Row 44: K14, repeat cable pattern of Row 8, k6.

Row 46: K14, repeat cable pattern of Row 10, k6.

Row 48: K7, M1, k7, repeat cable pattern of Row 12, k6–39 sts.

Row 50: K15, repeat cable pattern of Row 14, k3, M1, k3–40 sts.

Row 52: K15, repeat cable pattern of Row 16, k7.

Row 54: K15, repeat cable pattern of Row 6, k7.

Row 56: K15, repeat cable pattern of Row 8, k7.

Row 58: K15, repeat cable pattern of Row 10, k7.

Row 59: K1, *p2, k2; repeat from * to last stitch, k1.

Row 60: Knit.

Row 61: Repeat Row 59.

Row 62: Repeat Row 60. Bind off in rib pattern.

Right Wrist Warmer

Cast on 34 stitches.

Row 1 (WS): *K2, p2; repeat from * to last 2 stitches, k2.

Row 2: Knit.

Rows 3 and 4: Repeat Rows 1 and 2.

Row 5: P4, M1, p4, M1, p4, (k2, p2) 4 times, k2, M1 purlwise, p2, M1, p2–38 sts.

Row 6 (RS): K6, [(p2, T3F, T3B) twice, p2], k14.

Row 7 and all WS rows: Knit the knit stitches and purl the purl stitches as they appear.

Finish as for Left Wrist Warmer, except begin with k6 and end with k14.

FINISHING

Sew side seam, leaving a gap large enough for your thumb. Weave in ends.

Neck Warmer

Cast on 108 stitches.

Row 1 (RS): *P1, k2, p4, C4B, p4, k2, p4, C4F, p4, C4F, p3; repeat from * to end.

Row 2 and all WS rows through 12: Knit the knit stitches and purl

the purl stitches as they appear.

Row 3: *P1, (T3F, p2, T3B) twice, p1, (p2, T3B, T3F) twice, p2; repeat from * to end.

Row 5: *(P2, T3F, T3B) twice, p3, (T3B, p2, T3F) twice, p1; repeat from * to end.

Row 7: *P3, C4F, p4, C4F, p4, k2, p4, C4B, p4, k2, p1; repeat from * to end.

Row 9: *(P2, T3B, T3F) twice, p3, (T3F, p2, T3B) twice, p1; repeat from * to end.

Row 11: *P1, (T3B, p2, T3F) twice, p3, (T3F, T3B, p2) twice; repeat from * to end.

Repeat Rows 1–12 two more times, then repeat Row 1 once more. Bind off in pattern.

FINISHING

Sew side seam. Weave in ends.

• TID-BITE •

The hugely popular BUFFY THE VAMPIRE SLAYER about a teenage girl fighting the forces of evil was conceived as a gender-bending reversal of the traditional girl-victim. Beautiful and blonde, Buffy alone possesses the strength and skill to slay vampires and no male, demon or human, can beat her.

Silver Bullet-and-Blood Head Scarf

The purity of silver is considered toxic to vampires. With this beautiful scarf, you'll add a hint of sparkle to your wardrobe and keep the evil powers at bay at the same time.

DESIGNED BY → Tanis Gray   SKILL LEVEL → Easy

SIZE
One size

FINISHED MEASUREMENTS
Approximately 6" x 67" (15cm x 170cm), after blocking

MATERIALS
Filatura Di Crosa/Tahki Stacy Charles Zara (3) light (100% extra fine merino superwash; 1¾ oz/50g, 137 yd/125m): 1 skein in 1466 Red (A) → Filatura Di Crosa/Tahki Stacy Charles New Smoking (4) medium (65% viscose:, 35% polyester; .88 oz/25g, 131 yd/120m): 1 skein in 2 Silver (B) → Size 6 (4mm) straight needles → Tapestry needle

GAUGE
16 stitches and 37 rows = 4" (10cm) in garter stitch

Scarf
With A, cast on 25 stitches.
Next row: Slip first stitch purlwise, knit to end. Change to B.
Row 1 (RS): Slip first stitch purlwise, kfb, knit to last 3 stitches, k2tog, k1.
Row 2: Slip first stitch purlwise, knit to end. Change to A.
Repeat Rows 1 and 2 for pattern, changing colors every two rows, until piece measures approximately 67" (170cm), ending with A and Row 1.
Bind off knitwise.

Finishing
Weave in ends. Block.

Bellissima Mittens

These warm, wooly mittens were inspired by the mittens Bella wears in the movie TWILIGHT, just before Edward saves her life…the first time.

DESIGNED BY → Bethe Galantino  SKILL LEVEL → Intermediate

SIZE
Woman's S (M, L)

FINISHED MEASUREMENTS
Small: Approximately 7" (18cm) circumference

Medium: Approximately 7¾" (20cm) circumference

Large: Approximately 8½" (22cm) circumference

MATERIALS
Lamb's Pride Bulky **(5)** bulky (85% wool 15% mohair; 4 oz/113g, 125 yd/114m): 2 skeins in M04 Charcoal Heather

For Small: Set of 4 size 9 (5.5mm) double-pointed needles

For Medium: Set of 4 size 10 (6mm) double-pointed needles

For Large: Set of 4 size 10½ (6.5mm) double-pointed needles

→ Stitch markers → Waste yarn or stitch holder → Cable needle → Tapestry needle

GAUGE
Small: 14 stitches and 18 rows = 4" (10cm) in stockinette stitch

Medium: 13 stitches and 17 rows = 4" (10cm) in stockinette stitch

Large: 12 stitches and 16 rows = 4" (10cm) in stockinette stitch

SPECIAL SKILLS
→ **Cables (page 134)**

SPECIAL INSTRUCTIONS
→ **C6F:** Slip 3 stitches to cable needle and hold to front, k3, k3 from cable needle.

→ **C6B:** Slip 3 stitches to cable needle and hold to back, k3, k3 from cable needle.

→ **Kfb:** Knit in the front and back of the same stitch.

→ **M1R:** From the back, lift loop between stitches with the left needle, knit into front of loop.

→ **M1L:** From the front, lift loop between stitches with the left needle, knit into back of loop.

→ **TW2R:** K2tog (do not remove from left needle), swing needle around and knit the first stitch, then move stitches to the right-hand needle.

→ **TW2L:** From the back, knit the 2nd stitch on the needle through the back of the loop, swing needle around to the front and knit the first stitch through the front of the loop. Move both stitches to right-hand needle.

· TID-BITE ·

In almost all vampire stories, vampires have an aversion to sunlight, although not all of them die when exposed to the sun. In modern stories like TWILIGHT by Stephenie Meyer, the vampires sparkle in the sun and in THE VAMPIRE DIARIES by L.J. Smith, the Salvatore brothers wear a special ring that keeps them from burning up in the sun's rays.

STITCH PATTERNS

1X1 BIAS RIBBING

Rounds 1-4: *K1, p1; repeat from * to last stitch, end k1.

Round 5: K2tog, *k1, p1; repeat from * to last stitch, kfb.

Round 6: K2tog, *(p1, k1), repeat from * to last stitch, kfb.

Repeat Rounds 1-6 for pattern.

HORSESHOE CABLE PANEL

Rounds 1-4: P1, k12, p1.

Round 5: P1, C6F, C6B, p1.

Round 6: P1, k12, p1.

Repeat Rounds 1-6 for pattern.

Note: All sizes are worked the same, using different size needles to obtain finished size.

Cuff

With desired needle size, cast on 37 stitches. Place marker and join in the round, being careful not to twist the stitches.

Distribute stitches as follows:

Needle 1: 14 stitches

Needle 2: 11 stitches

Needle 3: 12 stitches

Knit 1 round.

Purl 1 round.

ESTABLISH PATTERN

Needle 1: Horseshoe Cable Panel.

Needles 2 and 3: 1x1 Bias Ribbing pattern.

Note: As Bias Ribbing pattern progresses, you will need to shift stitches between Needles 2 and 3 to compensate for increases and decreases in stitch pattern. Work 4-5 repeats of the Horseshoe Cable Panel to desired cuff length.

Left Mitten

Round 1: P1, k12, p1, k3 (move these 3 stitches to Needle 1), [k2tog, k2] 4 times, k1. There will be 3 stitches left; move these 3 stitches to Needle 1–new beginning of round–33 stitches.

New Stitch Distribution:

Needle 1: 20 stitches

Needle 2: 7 stitches

Needle 3: 6 stitches

Needles 2 and 3 will now be in stockinette stitch.

THUMB GUSSET

Round 2: P1, TW2R, p1, k12, p1, TW2L, p1, k10, M1R, pm, k1, M1L, k2.

Round 3: P1, k2, p1, k12, p1, k2, p1, knit to end of round.

Round 4: P1, TW2R, p1, k12, p1, TW2L, p1, knit to end of round.

Round 5: P1, k2, p1, C6F, C6B, p1, k2, p1, k11, M1R, sm, k1, M1L, knit to end of round.

Round 6: P1, TW2R, p1, k12, p1, TW2L, p1, knit to end of round.

Round 7: P1, k2, p1, k12, p1, k2, p1, knit to end of round.

Round 8: P1, TW2R, p1, k12, p1, TW2L, p1, k12, M1R, sm, k1, M1L, knit to end of round.

Round 9: P1, k2, p1, k12, p1, k2, p1, knit to end of round.

Round 10: P1, TW2R, p1, k12, p1, TW2L, p1, knit to end of round.

Round 11: P1, k2, p1, C6F, C6B, p1, k2, p1, k13, M1R, sm, k1, M1L, knit to end of round.

Round 12: P1, TW2R, p1, k12, p1, TW2L, p1, knit to end of round.

Round 13: P1, k2, p1, k12, p1, k2, p1, knit to end of round.

Round 14: P1, TW2R, p1, k12, p1, TW2L, p1, k14, M1R, sm, k1, M1L, knit to end of round–43 stitches.

Round 15: P1, k2, p1, k12, p1, k2, p1, k10, slip 10 gusset stitches to waste yarn, cast on 1 stitch over gap using backward loop method, knit to end of round–34 stitches.

HAND

Rounds 16-30: Continue in pattern as established.

Round 31: P1, k2, p1, [k1, ssk] 2 times, [k2tog, k1] 2 times, p1, k2, p1, knit to the end of the round.

Round 32: P1, TW2R, p1, k8, p1, TW2L, p1, knit to the end of the round.

Round 33: P1, k2, p1, k1, k2tog, k2, ssk, k1, p1, k2, p1, knit to the end of the round.

Round 34: P1, TW2L, p1, k2tog, k2, ssk, p1, TW2L, p1, k1, ssk, knit to last 3 stitches, k2tog, k1.

Round 35: P1, k2, p1, ssk, k2tog, p1, k2, p1, k1, ssk, knit to last 3 stitches, k2tog, k1.

Round 36: P1, k1, ssk, k2, k2tog, k1, p1, k1, ssk, knit to last 3 stitches, k2tog, k1.

Round 37: P1, ssk, k2, k2tog, p1, k1, ssk, knit to last 3 stitches, k2tog, k1.

Round 38: P1, ssk, k2tog, p1, k1, ssk, k2tog, k1—8 stitches.

Break yarn, pull through remaining stitches to close the top of the mitten.

Right Mitten

Make cuff same as for Left Mitten.

Round 1: P1, k12, p1, k3 (move these 3 stitches to needle 1), [k2tog, k2] 4 times, k1.

There will be 3 stitches left; move these 3 stitches to Needle 1—new beginning of round—33 stitches.

New Stitch Distribution:

Needle 1: 20 stitches

Needle 2: 7 stitches

Needle 3: 6 stitches

Needles 2 and 3 will now be in stockinette stitch.

THUMB GUSSET

Round 2: P1, TW2R, p1, k12, p1, TW2L, p1, k2, M1R, pm, k1, M1L, knit to the end of the round.

Round 3: P1, k2, p1, k12, p1, k2, p1, knit to the end of the round.

Round 4: P1, TW2R, p1, k12, p1, TW2L, p1, knit to the end of the round.

Round 5: P1, k2, p1, C6F, C6B, p1, k2, p1, k3, M1R, sm, k1, M1L, knit to end of round.

Round 6: P1, TW2R, p1, k12, p1, TW2L, p1, knit to the end of the round.

Round 7: P1, k2, p1, k12, p1, k2, p1, knit to the end of the round.

Round 8: P1, TW2R, p1, k12, p1, TW2L, p1, k4, M1R, sm, k1, M1L, knit to the end of the round.

Round 9: P1, k2, p1, k12, p1, k2, p1, knit to the end of the round.

Round 10: P1, TW2R, p1, k12, p1, TW2L, p1, knit to the end of the round.

Round 11: P1, k2, p1, C6F, C6B, p1, k2, p1, k5, M1R, sm, k1, M1L, knit to the end of the round.

Round 12: P1, TW2R, p1, k12, p1, TW2L, p1, knit to the end of the round.

Round 13: P1, k2, p1, k12, p1, k2, p1, knit to the end of the round.

Round 14: P1, TW2R, p1, k12, p1, TW2L, p1, k6, M1R, sm, k1, M1L, knit to the end of the round—43 stitches.

Round 15: P1, k2, p1, k12, p1, k2, p1, k2, slip 10 stitches to waste yarn, cast on 1 stitch using backward loop method, knit to the end of the round—34 stitches.

HAND

Rounds 16-30: Continue in pattern as established.

Round 31: P1, k2, p1, [k1, ssk] 2 times, [k2tog, k1] 2 times, p1, k2, p1, knit to the end of the round.

Round 32: P1, TW2R, p1, k8, p1, TW2L, p1, knit to the end of the round.

Round 33: P1, k2, p1, k1, k2tog, k2, ssk, k1, p1, k2, p1, knit to the end of the round.

Round 34: P1, TW2R, p1, k2tog, k2, ssk, p1, TW2L, p1, k1, ssk, knit to the last 3 stitches, k2tog, k1.

Round 35: P1, k2, p1, ssk, k2tog, p1, k2, p1, k1, ssk, knit to the last 3 stitches, k2tog, k1.

Round 36: P1, k1, ssk, k2, k2tog, k1, p1, k1, ssk, knit to the last 3 stitches, k2tog, k1.

Round 37: P1, ssk, k2, k2tog, p1, k1, ssk, knit to the last 3 stitches, k2tog, k1.

Round 38: P1, ssk, k2tog, p1, k1, ssk, k2tog, k1—8 stitches.

Break yarn, pull through remaining stitches to close top of mitten.

THUMB (BOTH MITTENS)

Move the first 2 stitches from the waste yarn to the first needle, place the next 4 stitches on a second needle, and the final 4 on a third needle. With the fourth needle, pick up 2 stitches over the gap and knit the 2 stitches from Needle 1—12 stitches.

Continue to knit around until only the tip of your thumb peeks over the top or approximately 1½" (4cm).

Decrease round: *K2tog, knit to end of needle; repeat from * for each needle.

Knit one round even. Repeat decrease round one more time. Break yarn; pull yarn through the remaining stitches to close the top of the thumb.

Finishing

Weave in ends.

Under Cover of Midnight Hooded Cowl

There is no better protection from bloodthirsty vampires than this plush hooded cowl, which encircles your delicate and appetizing human neck with warm woolen cables. Worn as hood, it will help you blend into the shadows.

DESIGNED BY → Julie Turjoman   SKILL LEVEL → Intermediate

SIZE
One size

FINISHED MEASUREMENTS
18" x 32" (circumference at bottom edge) (46cm x 81cm)

MATERIALS
KnitPicks Cadena **5** bulky (70% wool, 30% alpaca, 3½ oz/100g, 110 yds/100m): 4 skeins in Admiral → Size 10½ (6.5mm) 16" and 24" circular needles → Stitch markers → Cable needle → Tapestry needle

GAUGE
14 stitches and 18 rows = 4" (10cm) in stockinette stitch

SPECIAL SKILLS
→ **Cables (page 134)**

SPECIAL INSTRUCTIONS
→ **C6F:** Place 3 stitches on cable needle and hold to front, k3, k3 from cable needle.
→ **C6B:** Place 3 stitches on cable needle and hold to back, k3, k3 from cable needle.

STITCH PATTERNS
SEED STITCH (worked over an odd number of stitches)
Round 1: *K1, p1; repeat from * to end.
Round 2: *P1, k1; repeat from * to end.
Repeat Rounds 1 and 2 for pattern.

GRADUATED 9-STITCH BRAIDED CABLE
Graduated cable lengths are created by working 5 rounds even between cable crossing rounds twice, then 4 rounds even between cable crossing rounds twice, then 3 rounds even between cable crossing rounds to the end.

NOTE
Change to shorter circular needle when needed.

· TID-BITE ·

Miriam Blaylock, a character played by Catherine Deneuve in the 1983 movie THE HUNGER, was a dangerous beauty who draws in human lovers, offering them eternal life—until she's through with them and then they're left to deteriorate and wither away.

Cowl

With longer circular needles, cast on 143 stitches. Place marker and join in a round, being careful not to twist the stitches. Work in seed stitch for 4 rounds.

Next round (cable set-up): M1 purlwise (p1, k1 in same st), p6, *pm, k9, pm, p7, repeat from * to end of round, ending with k9–144 stitches, 7 stitches in each purl section.

Work 2 rounds even in pattern.

Cable Repeat:

Next round (cable round 1): *P7, C6B, k3; repeat from * around. Work 5 rounds even in pattern.

Next round (cable round 2): *P7, k3, C6F; repeat from * around. Work 5 rounds even in pattern. Work Cable Repeat once more. AT THE SAME TIME, when piece measures 4" (10cm), decrease 9 stitches evenly across next round in the purl sections, as follows: *p3, p2tog, p2, work cable crossing or knit stitches depending on round; repeat from * around–135 stitches, 6 stitches in each purl section. Work Cable Repeat twice more, working 4 rounds even instead of 5 between cable rounds.

Work Cable Repeat to end, working 3 rounds even instead of 4 between cable rounds.

AT THE SAME TIME, decrease 9 stitches evenly around in purl sections every 2" (5cm) 4 times more, as follows:

Decrease Round 1: *P2, p2tog, p2, work cable crossing or knit stitches depending on round; repeat from * around–126 stitches, 5 stitches in each purl section.

Decrease Round 2: *P2, p2tog, p1, work cable crossing or knit stitches depending on round; repeat from * around–117 stitches, 4 stitches in each purl section.

Decrease Round 3: *P1, p2tog, p1, work cable crossing or knit stitches depending on round; repeat from * around–108 stitches, 3 stitches in each purl section.

Decrease Round 4: *P2tog, p1, work cable crossing or knit stitches depending on round; repeat from * around–99 stitches, 2 stitches in each purl section.

Continue in pattern until cowl measures 17½" (44cm) long. Work in seed stitch for 4 rounds. Bind off loosely in pattern.

Finishing

Weave in ends. Block lightly.

Vampire Diary Protector

If you keep a diary, like L.J. Smith's Elena or Stefan, you can keep your thoughts private with this beautiful protector. No one will know that your deepest, darkest secrets hide inside.

DESIGNED BY → Stephanie Spiers   SKILL LEVEL → Intermediate

SIZE
Fits a book or day journal 5" x 8" x ½" (13cm x 20cm x 1 cm)

FINISHED MEASUREMENTS
Approximately 8½" x 10½" (22cm x 27cm), opened flat

MATERIALS
Patons Classic Wool 4 medium (100% wool; 3½ oz/100g, 223 yd/205m): 1 skein in Winter White → Size 5 (3.75mm) straight needles → Cable needle → Tapestry needle → Spiral-bound day planner or journal, 5" x 8" x ½" (13cm x 20cm x 1 cm) → 2 yd (1.8m) red ribbon, ½" (1.27cm) wide

GAUGE
23 sts and 33 rows = 4" (10cm) in Linen Stitch

SPECIAL SKILLS
→ **Cables (page 134)**

SPECIAL INSTRUCTIONS
→ **C6F:** Place 3 stitches on cable needle and hold to front, k3, k3 from cable needle.

→ **C6B:** Place 3 stitches on cable needle and hold to back, k3, k3 from cable needle.

STITCH PATTERN
LINEN STITCH
Row 1 (RS): *K1, slip next stitch purlwise while holding yarn in front; repeat from * across.
Row 2: Purl.
Row 3: *Slip next stitch purlwise while holding yarn in front, k1; repeat from * across.
Row 4: Purl.
Repeat Rows 1-4 for pattern.

· TID-BITE ·

Fact or fiction? The 2000 movie SHADOW OF THE VAMPIRE starring Willem Dafoe as Max Shreck puts a new twist on vampire movies. The movie shows just how frightening it could be if the actor portraying the undead really IS what he portrays.

Diary Cover

Cast on 88 stitches.

Row 1 (RS): P1, *p1, k12, p1, work in Linen Stitch over next 10 stitches; repeat from * 2 times more, p1, k12, p2.

Row 2: K1, *k1, p12, k1, p10; repeat from * 2 times more, k1, p12, k2.

Row 3-4: Repeat Rows 1 and 2.

Row 5: P1, *p1, C6B, C6F, p1, work in Linen Stitch over next 10 stitches; repeat from * 2 times more, p1, C6B, C6F, p2.

Row 6-12: Repeat Row 2 on all even rows and repeat Row 1 on all odd rows.

Row 13: Repeat Row 5.

Rows 14-69: Repeat Row 2 on all even rows and repeat Row 1 on all odd rows EXCEPT Rows 21, 29, 37, 45, 53, 61 and 69, which should be worked as Row 5.

Bind off.

Finishing

TOP AND BOTTOM FLAPS (MAKE 4)

Cast on 26 stitches. Work in stockinette stitch for 6 rows. Bind off.

Sew these flaps to the top and bottom of the cover. Start at the outermost edge and work the sewing inward so the flap covers approximately the area of 2 cable panels and 1 linen stitch panel on each side (center will be left open for spine). Be sure to pinch in the cables on the top and bottom of the cover while sewing to give them more definition.

SIDE FLAPS

With RS facing, pick up and knit 28 stitches along the side, beginning 1" (2.5cm) below the top edge and ending 1" (2.5cm) above the bottom, so that edges of side flap will touch top and bottom flaps when folded down. Work in stockinette stitch for 6 rows. Bind off. Repeat on the opposite side. Sew the edges of the flaps together to fit over the edges of the book. Weave in ends and block flat.

RIBBON

Using a tapestry needle, weave in ribbon through the cables along Rows 13 and 61 as shown. Secure ribbon underneath flaps. If desired, use extra ribbon to help secure the cover near the book spine to prevent curling and to use as a bookmark.

· TID-BITE ·

DRACUL means "the dragon" or "the devil" in Romanian and is where the name Dracula (for Vlad II, ruler of Wallachia,) comes from.

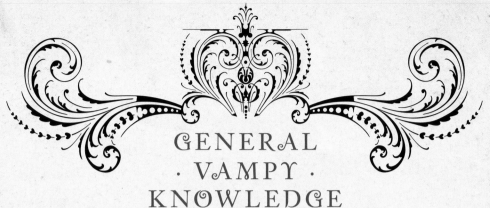

GENERAL · VAMPY · KNOWLEDGE

So you think you're in the know? Take this quiz and find out how much of a vamp you really are!

1 When a vampire turns a human into a vampire, the relationship between the two is called:

a) Master and servant
b) Maker and made
c) Parent and child
d) Master and apprentice

2 The oldest vampire legends tell of ugly, bloated, scary creatures full of blood they'd just drunk. It wasn't until which story was told that we began to romanticize vampires in literature?

a) *Dracula* by Bram Stoker
b) *The Vampyre* by John Polidori
c) *Interview With The Vampire* by Anne Rice
d) *Twilight* by Stephenie Meyer
e) *Carmilla* by Sheridan Le Fanu

3 All of these are names for groups of vampires except which one?

a) Clutch
b) Coven
c) Pack
d) Family
e) Nest

4 From what country did the origins of the vampire-to-bat legend come from?

a) Romania
b) India
c) America
d) Brazil

5 The legend of the Langsuir, about a woman who died in childbirth and takes revenge by terrorizing villages and sucking blood from a hole in the back of her neck, comes from what country's folklore?

a) India
b) Italy
c) Malaysia
d) Bulgaria
e) Russia

6 The Russian word UPIR, which translates to "vampire," was first used in a document in what year?

a) 1750
b) 1047
c) 1890
d) 1475

Love Bites—for Him

Knit this comfy sweater for your favorite vampire-loving Goth boy. Knit in all black, the dropped stitches give it a worn and torn look—perfect for chilly nights out on the town.

DESIGNED BY → Toni Carr   SKILL LEVEL → Intermediate

SIZE
Men's S (M, L, XL)

FINISHED MEASUREMENTS
Chest: 38 (40, 42½, 44½)" [97 (102, 108, 113)cm]

MATERIALS
KnitPicks Wool of the Andes **(4)** medium (100% wool; 1¾ oz/50g, 110 yd/100m): 9 (9, 10, 11) skeins in Coal → Size 8 (5mm) 29" circular needle → Stitch marker → Waste yarn → Tapestry needle → Four 1" (2.5cm) buttons

GAUGE
20 sts and 26 rows = 4" (10cm) in stockinette stitch

NOTE
The dropped stitches are supposed to look random and imperfect, so feel free to change their position or add more if desired.

Front

Cast on 190 (200, 212, 222) stitches. Place marker and join in the round. Place a second marker 95 (100, 106, 111) stitches away to mark opposite side "seam". Work even in stockinette stitch for 3" (8cm).

Next round: K75 (85, 97, 107), drop next stitch, yo, knit to end.

Next round: K20 (30, 42, 52) drop next stitch and allow to unravel, yo, k10, drop next stitch, yo, k50, drop next stitch, yo, knit to the end of the round.

Work even in stockinette stitch for 10 rounds.

Work even in stockinette stitch until piece measures 17 (17, 17½, 18)" [43 (43, 44, 46)cm].

DIVIDE FOR ARMHOLES

Knit to first marker, place next 95 (100, 106, 111) stitches on waste yarn for Back.

· TID-BITE ·

A cult favorite, FOREVER KNIGHT, which ran from 1992 to 1996, was the story of Nick Knight, an 800-year-old vampire working in present-day Toronto as a homicide detective trying to make amends for his former bloodsucking life.

SHAPE ARMHOLES (FRONT)

Working on remaining 95 (100, 106, 111) stitches, bind off 6 (6, 8, 10) stitches at beginning of next 2 rows—83 (88, 90, 91) stitches.

Next row (RS): Decrease 1 stitch at each end of the row.

Next row: Purl.

Repeat last 2 rows once more—79 (84, 86, 87) stitches. Work even in stockinette stitch until armholes measure 8 (8, 8½, 9)" [20 (20, 22, 23)cm], ending with a wrong-side row.

SHAPE SHOULDERS

Bind off 19 (21, 22, 22) stitches at beginning of next 2 rows—41 (42, 42, 43) stitches. Place remaining stitches on waste yarn for neck.

Back

Work as for Front.

Neck

Place held neck stitches on needles. Working back and forth in rows, work in stockinette stitch for 8 rows. Bind off loosely.

Sew shoulder seams and open edge of neck.

Sleeves (make 2)

Cast on 58 (60, 64, 68) stitches. Work in stockinette stitch for 6 rows, ending with a wrong-side row.

Row 7 (RS): K3, bind off 3 stitches

for buttonhole, knit to the end of the row.

Row 8: Purl to last 3 stitches, cast on 3 stitches over gap to close buttonhole, p3.

Row 9: K12(14, 16, 18), drop next stitch and allow to ravel, yo, knit to the end of the row.

Row 10: Purl.

Row 11: K20(26, 30, 34), drop next stitch, yo, knit to the end of the row.

Row 12: Purl.

Row 13: Knit.

Row 14: Purl.

Row 15: Repeat Row 7.

Row 16: Repeat Row 8.

Row 17: K36 (42, 46, 50), drop next stitch, yo, knit to the end of the row.

Row 18: Purl.

Row 19: Knit.

Row 20: Purl.

Row 21: K25 (28, 32, 34), drop next stitch, yo, knit to the end of the row.

Row 22: P8 (10, 14, 16), drop next stitch, yo, purl to the end of the row.

Work even in stockinette stitch until sleeve measures 13 (13, 13½, 14)" [33 (33, 34, 36)cm], ending with a wrong-side row.

SHAPE SLEEVE

Next row (RS): K1, M1, knit to the last stitch, M1, k1.

Next row: Purl.

Repeat last 2 rows 11 (12, 13, 11) times [80 (84, 90, 90) stitches]. Work even in stockinette stitch until the piece measures 18" (46cm).

SHAPE CAP

Bind off 6 (6, 8, 10) stitches at the beginning of the next 2 rows. Decrease 1 stitch at each end

of row every right side row 2 times—64 (68, 70, 66) stitches. Size XL only, work even for 4 rows. Decrease 1 stitch at each end of every row until 16 stitches remain. Bind off 2 stitches at the beginning of next 4 rows. Bind off remaining 8 stitches.

Finishing

Seam sleeves, leaving seam open from edge of cuff to just above buttonholes. Set in sleeves and seam. Weave in ends. Sew buttons opposite buttonholes.

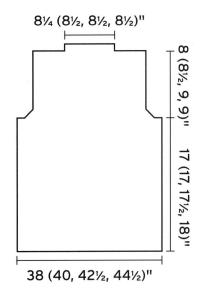

8¼ (8½, 8½, 8½)"

8 (8½, 9, 9)"

17 (17, 17½, 18)"

38 (40, 42½, 44½)"

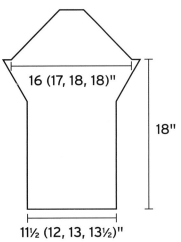

16 (17, 18, 18)"

18"

11½ (12, 13, 13½)"

2

JUST BITTEN

You've just been awakened from slumber to find you're incredibly thirsty. You're covered in blood, and you don't think it's your own. If you had a heartbeat, it would quicken, but you notice your chest is strangely silent and calm. Your senses are heightened, and you have an unfamiliar urge to go on a rampage. Newly turned vampires are commonly thought to be the most dangerous. Ruled by their thirst, they have to say goodbye to their former life as a human as they enter into the darker world of the undead. They're not yet used to their hunger or newfound strength, and often go on rampages, draining innocent lives along the way.

In this chapter are a tourniquet scarf and blood-drop socks for your new bloodsucking life, sexy fishnet gloves perfect for a newly-turned vamp, a wrap symbolizing your descent into a dark life, and a hooded coat for covering up when you're ready to slink out

Tourniquet Scarf

Make yourself a willing vampire victim with this scarf. Knit with red in the middle and embellished with "dripping blood," this vampy scarf can serve a dual purpose: neck warmer and tourniquet.

DESIGNED BY → Genevieve Miller   SKILL LEVEL → Easy

SIZE
One size fits all

FINISHED MEASUREMENTS
Approximately 5" x 86" (13cm x 218cm)

MATERIALS
Plymouth Encore Worsted (4) medium (75% acrylic, 25% wool; 3½ oz/100g, 200 yd/182m): 2 skeins in 520 Charcoal Heather [MC] and 1 skein in 9601 Red [CC] → Plymouth Encore DK (3) light (75% acrylic, 25% wool; 1¾ oz/50g, 150 yd/137m): 1 skein in 9601 Red for duplicate stitch (optional) → Size 9 (5.5mm) straight needles → Tapestry needle

GAUGE
Gauge is not essential for this project.

SPECIAL SKILLS
→ **Stranded knitting (page 134)**

→ **Duplicate stitch (page 135)**

Scarf
With MC, cast on 40 stitches.
Work in stockinette stitch for 4 rows.
Next (picot) row (RS): K1, *yo, k2tog; repeat from * to last stitch, k1.
Work in k2, p2 rib until piece measures 26" (66cm), ending with a wrong side row.
Join CC.

Next row (RS): *K1 in MC, k1 in CC, p1 in MC, p1 in CC; repeat from * across, carrying both strands of yarn together along the back of the piece. Work as established for 3 more rows. Cut MC.
With CC, work in k2, p2 rib for 32" (81cm), ending with a wrong side row.
Join MC.
Next row (RS): *K1 in MC, k1 in CC, p1 in MC, p1 in CC; repeat from * across, carrying both strands of yarn together along the back of the piece. Work as established for 3 more rows. Cut CC.
With MC, work in k2, p2 rib for 25" (64cm) more, ending with a wrong side row.
Next (picot) row (RS): K1, *yo, k2tog; repeat from * to last stitch, k1.
Work in stockinette stitch for 3 rows. Bind off knitwise.

Finishing
Weave in ends. Block after working duplicate stitch.

EMBELLISHMENT (OPTIONAL)
Using CC or DK weight yarn in contrasting color, use duplicate stitch to create a dripping blood effect at both ends of the CC section as shown. You can make it as dramatic or subtle as you like so your scarf is truly one of a kind. If you do opt for the embellishment, blocking the scarf will make it look more polished.

Rampage Fishnet Gloves

Black fishnets for sexy vampires! Long ago in eastern Europe, people would hang fishnets over their doors to keep vampires from entering. They believed vampires had a compulsive need to untie knots, so the vampires would be distracted by the knots in the fishnets for hours.

DESIGNED BY → Kimberly Dijkstra   SKILL LEVEL → Intermediate

SIZE
One size fits most

FINISHED MEASUREMENTS
Approximately 5" circumference x 8" long (6cm x 20cm), unstretched
Approximately 7½" circumference x 12" long (10cm x 30cm), stretched

MATERIALS
Elann Esprit (2) fine (98.3% cotton, 1.7% elastic; 1¾ oz/50g), 100 yd/91m): 1 skein in Black → Size 8 (5mm) circular or set of 4 double-pointed needles → Size 13 (9mm) needles (for bind off) → Stitch marker → ¼" (0.5cm) wide braided elastic (optional) → 2½ yd (2.28m) of ⅞" (2cm) wide satin ribbon (optional) → Tapestry needle

GAUGE
Approximately 20 stitches and 26 rows = 4" (10cm), unstretched
Approximately 12 stitches and 18 rows = 4" (10cm), stretched

SPECIAL INSTRUCTIONS

→ **Dtk (double twisted knit):**
Insert needle into stitch knitwise, bring yarn up from under the right-hand needle between the two needles, wrap the yarn around the left-hand needle, over the top of both needles, and around the right-hand needle. Then knit the stitch by bringing the yarn wrapped around the right-hand needle beneath and clear of the crossed strands on the left-hand needle. These strands are dropped off the left-hand needle as the stitch is completed.

→ **Dtp (double twisted purl):**
Insert needle into stitch purlwise, make a backwards loop, place it on the right-hand needle and tighten. Bring the loop through the stitch like any other purl stitch.

NOTES
Use either the Magic Loop method (page 40) or double-pointed needles for working in the round.
The double twisted knit stitch involves making a "figure 8" over the needles before drawing the yarn through the stitch. With a bit of practice, it will become as natural as making a regular knit stitch.
These gloves are very stretchy due to the stitch pattern and the elasticity of the yarn. The gloves may look small on the needles, but once finished, they will stretch and conform to your arms, revealing the grid pattern.

Cuff

Cast on 23 stitches very loosely. Place marker and join in the round, being careful not to twist the stitches.

Rounds 1-47: *Dtk; repeat from * around.

THUMB OPENING

Turn.

Row 48 (WS): Dtp across 23 stitches, turn.

Row 49: Dtk back across 23 stitches.

TOP OF HAND

Resume working in the round.

Rounds 50-53: *Dtk; repeat from * around.

Right Glove

Bind off using larger needles as follows:

K2, slip both stitches back to left-hand needle, k2tog tbl, [k1, slip 2 stitches back to left-hand needle, k2tog tbl] 11 times, pick up 8th bound-off stitch with right-hand needle, k1, slip 3 stitches back to left-hand needle, k3tog tbl, [k1, slip 2 stitches back to left-hand needle, k2tog tbl] 2 times, pick up 6th bound-off stitch with right-hand needle, k1, slip 3 stitches back to left-hand needle, k3tog tbl, [k1, slip 2 stitches back to left-hand needle, k2tog tbl] 3 times, pick up 4th bound-off stitch with right-hand needle, k1, slip 3 stitches back to

left-hand needle, k3tog tbl, [k1, slip 2 stitches back to left-hand needle, k2tog tbl] 2 times. Fasten off. Weave in ends.

Left Glove

Bind off using larger needles as follows:

K2, slip both stitches back to left-hand needle, k2tog tbl, [k1, slip 2 stitches back to left-hand needle, k2tog tbl] 13 times, pick up 10th bound-off stitch with right-hand needle, k1, slip 3 stitches back to left-hand needle, k3tog tbl, k1, slip 2 stitches back to left-hand needle, k2tog tbl, pick up 7th bound-off stitch with right-hand needle, k1, slip 3 stitches back to left-hand needle, k3tog tbl, k1, slip 2 stitches back to left-hand needle, k2tog tbl, pick up 3rd bound-off stitch with right-hand needle, k1, slip 3 stitches back to left-hand needle, k3tog tbl, [k1, slip 2 stitches back

to left-hand needle, k2tog tbl] 3 times. Fasten off. Weave in ends.

Finishing (optional)

Stitch elastic to inside of cast-on row of each glove. Weave ribbon through Round 1 and tie in a bow.

· TID-BITE ·

Although modern-day vampires are usually portrayed as pale, in folkloric tales of old they were often bloated and ruddy from having fed on human blood.

· MAGIC LOOP ·

With the Magic Loop method, you can knit small circumferences on a circular needle. You will need a long circular needle with a very flexible cable. Cast on your stitches and slide them onto the cable. Find the center, and pull the cable out between the center two stitches. Slide your stitches back onto the needles and line them up next to each other. There should be the same number of stitches on each needle. Pull the right-hand needle out (these stitches will slide down onto the cable), being careful not to twist the stitches.

Begin knitting. When you reach the end of the row, slide the stitches that are on the cable up onto the needle and again pull out the right-hand needle to continue knitting.

Bloody Socks

Wear these socks with a stitch pattern that resembles droplets of blood to remind yourself of your obsession with vampires. If you are a fledgling vampire, wear them and keep your secret in plain sight.

DESIGNED BY ⇢ Kimberly Dijkstra   SKILL LEVEL ⇢ Experienced

SIZE
Women's Medium

FINISHED MEASUREMENTS
7¼" (18cm) in circumference

MATERIALS
Kraemer Sterling & Silk  super fine (63% superwash merino, 20% silk, 15% nylon, 2% silver; 3½ oz/100g, 420 yd/384m): 1 skein in Red Carpet ⇢ 2 pairs size 2 (2.75mm) circular needles ⇢ Stitch markers ⇢ Tapestry needle

GAUGE
32 stitches and 44 rows = 4" (10cm)

SPECIAL INSTRUCTIONS
⇢ **Provisional cast-on**
You'll use two strands of yarn—the knitting yarn and a strand of scrap yarn. Holding a knitting needle in your right hand, tie a slip-knot with the working yarn and scrap yarn, and slip the loop onto the knitting needle. Hold the scrap yarn to the back and the knitting yarn to the front of the needle. Wrap the working yarn around the knitting needle once. Then move the needle to the back of the scrap yarn and wrap the scrap yarn and the working yarn around the needle. Move the needle back to the original position and repeat, wrapping the yarn around it, alternating picking it up from the front and the back of the scrap yarn.

⇢ **Tubular bind-off**
Used for 1 x 1 ribbing, this bind-off is also quite stretchy. When you are finished knitting, cut a tail about four times the length of the edge you will be binding off. Thread this tail onto a tapestry needle. *Insert the needle into the first stitch knitwise (from left to right through the front loop), draw the yarn through, and drop the stitch from the knitting needle. Insert the needle purlwise (from right to left through front loop) into second stitch on the knitting needle, and draw the yarn through. Insert the needle purlwise through first stitch on knittting needle, draw the yarn through, and drop the stitch from the knitting needle. Insert the needle from back to front between the first two stitches and draw the yarn through. Insert the needle knitwise into the second stitch and draw the yarn through.* Repeat from * to * until all live stitches are bound off.

NOTE
The socks are knit from the toe up to the cuff.

· TID-BITE ·

The first vampire movie was a two-minute French silent film called LE MANOIR DU DIABLE (House of the Devil), directed by Georges Méliès and released in 1896. Though it was short and meant to entertain not frighten people, it is considered the first horror film.

Socks

Using a provisional cast-on with cable of the second circular needle instead of scrap yarn, cast on 16 stitches (8 stitches per needle). Work in the round.

TOE

Rounds 1 and 2: Knit, working twisted stitches through the back loop to untwist on first round.
Round 3: *K1, M1, knit to last st, M1, k1; repeat from * on 2nd needle (4 stitches increased).
Round 4: Knit.
Rounds 5-22: Repeat Rounds 3 and 4–56 stitches total, 28 stitches on each needle.
Round 23: *M1, knit to end; repeat from * on 2nd needle–58 stitches.
Round 24: Knit.

FOOT

Rounds 25-27: Purl stitches on Needle 1 (instep); knit stitches on Needle 2 (sole).
Round 28 (Row 1 of chart): P2, [yo, p2tog, p4] 4 times, yo, p2tog, p1; knit sole stitches.
Rounds 29-32: P2, [k1, p5] 4 times, k1, p2; knit sole stitches.
Round 33: P2, [p1 tbl, p5] 4 times, p1 tbl, p2; knit sole stitches.
Round 34: P5, [yo, p2tog, p4] 4 times; knit sole stitches.
Rounds 35-38: [P5, k1] 4 times, p5; knit sole stitches.
Round 39: [P5, p1 tbl] 4 times, p5; knit sole stitches.

Repeat Rounds 28-39 until piece measures 2" (5cm) less than desired length of foot.

HEEL

Heel is worked on Needle 2 only. The 29 instep stitches on Needle 1 remain unworked until the gusset section.

HEEL FLAP

Row 1 (WS): Sl 1, purl to end.
Row 2: Sl 1, knit to end.
Row 3: Sl 1, purl to end.
Repeat Rows 2 and 3 until the heel flap measures 2½" (6cm).

TURN HEEL

Row 1 (RS): Sl 1, k15, ssk, turn.
Row 2: Sl 1, p4, p2tog, p1, turn.
Row 3: Sl 1, k6, ssk, k1, turn.
Row 4: Sl 1, p7, p2tog, p1, turn.
Row 5: Sl 1, k8, ssk, k1, turn.
Continue as established until all stitches have been worked, ending with a wrong side row.

GUSSET

Needle 2: Knit 9 stitches, place marker, knit the remaining 8 stitches, pick up and knit 1 stitch in each of the slipped stitches along the edge of the heel flap and one additional stitch where the heel flap and instep meet, place marker, work 15 instep stitches in pattern.
Needle 1: Work remaining 14 instep stitches in pattern, place marker, pick up and knit one stitch where the instep and heel flap meet and one stitch in each of the slipped stitches along the edge of the heel flap, knit heel stitches to marker.

NOTES

Rounds now begin in the middle of the heel. There are 3 stitch markers—one to indicate the end of a round, and one on either side of the instep. Slip markers as you come to them.

GUSSET SHAPING

Round 1:
Needle 2: Knit to 2 stitches before marker, k2tog, work in pattern to end.
Needle 1: Knit in pattern to marker, ssk, knit to end.
Round 2:
Needle 2: Knit to marker, work in pattern to end.

Needle 1: Work in pattern to marker, knit to end.
Repeat these two rounds until 58 stitches remain (29 stitches on each needle). Transfer stitches so that Needle 1 holds all 29 instep stitches and Needle 2 holds 29 knit stitches. Remove markers.

LEG

Continue working in pattern on Needle 1 and knitting all stitches on Needle 2 until Row 9 of the chart is completed or the desired length. Purl all stitches on Needle 2 for next 3 rounds (Rows 10–12 of chart). Work Rows 1–6 of chart on both needles. Purl 1 round.

CUFF

Work in k1, p1 rib for 6 rounds. Cut yarn, leaving a tail four times longer than the circumference of the sock. Bind off using a tubular bind-off. Weave in ends.

Lace Chart

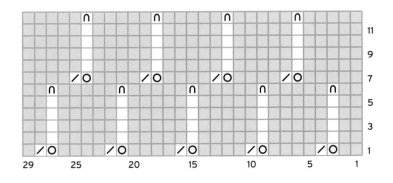

K				
P				
Yarn over	O			
P2tog	/			
Ptbl	∩			

Descent into Darkness Wrap

Make a wrap that symbolizes the descent into darkness fledgling vampires must make as they are forced to say goodbye to the golden hues of sunlight and live forever in the obscurity of darkness.

Designed by ⇢ Marilee Norris   Skill Level ⇢ Intermediate

SIZE
One size

FINISHED MEASUREMENTS
21" x 72" (53cm x 183cm)

MATERIALS
KnitPicks Swish Worsted (4) medium (100% superwash wool; 1¾ oz/50g, 110 yd/100m): 2 skeins each of Gold (A), Allspice (B), Copper (C), Truffle (D), Black (E) ⇢ Size 11 (8mm) straight needles ⇢ Tapestry needle ⇢ Gauge ⇢ 15 stitches and 18 rows = 4" (10cm) in stockinette stitch

SPECIAL INSTRUCTIONS
⇢ **Sl 1, k2tog, psso:** Slip 1 stitch purlwise, knit next 2 stitches together, pass slipped stitch over.

STITCH PATTERN
DIAGONAL LACE
Row 1 (RS): *K1, yo, sl 1, k2tog, psso, yo; repeat from * to last 2 stitches, k2.
Rows 2, 4, and 6: Purl.
Row 3: K2, *yo, sl 1, k2tog, psso, yo, k1; repeat from * to end.
Row 5: K2tog, yo, k1, yo, *sl 1, k2tog, psso, yo, k1, yo; repeat from * to last 3 stitches, ssk, k1.
Row 7: K1, k2tog, yo, k1, yo, *sl 1, k2tog, psso, yo, k1, yo; repeat from * to last 2 stitches, ssk.
Row 8: Purl.
Repeat Rows 1-8 for pattern.

Wrap
With A, cast on 82 stitches. Work 7 repeats (one repeat = Rows 1-8 of pattern) of Diagonal Lace pattern.
With B, work 1 pattern repeat.
With A, work 1 pattern repeat.
With B, work 7 pattern repeats.
With C, work 1 pattern repeat.
With B, work 1 pattern repeat.
With C, work 7 pattern repeats.
With D, work 1 pattern repeat.
With C, work 1 pattern repeat.
With D, work 7 pattern repeats.
With E, work 1 pattern repeat.
With D, work 1 pattern repeat.
With E, work 7 pattern repeats.
Bind off loosely.

Finishing
Weave in ends. Block if desired.

Lore Hoodie

Walk through misty woods shrouded in this evocative cardigan with its graceful lace skirt and generous hood. Knit in wool in a moody heathered berry shade, this alluring sweater coat is nearly seamless and surprisingly lightweight.

DESIGNED BY → Cirilia Rose   SKILL LEVEL → Intermediate

SIZE
Women's XS (S, M, L, XL)

FINISHED MEASUREMENTS
Bust: 32 (36, 40, 44, 48)" [81 (91, 101.5, 112, 122)cm]

GAUGE
12 stitches and 14 rows = 4" (10cm) in stockinette stitch using larger needles

MATERIALS
Berroco Peruvia Quick (4) medium (100% Peruvian Highland wool; 3½ oz/100g, 103yd/94m): 7 (8, 10, 10, 12) skeins in 9148 Boysenberry → Set of 5 size 10½ (6.5mm) double-pointed needles (or size needed to obtain gauge) → Size 11 (8mm) 32" circular needle → Size K-10.5 (6.5mm) crochet hook → Small amount of scrap yarn → Locking stitch markers → Tapestry needle → Sewing needle and matching thread → 4 buttons

SPECIAL INSTRUCTIONS
→ **M1R:** With tip of left needle, lift strand between needles from back to front; knit the lifted loop through the front.

→ **M1L:** With tip of left needle, lift strand between needles from front to back; knit the lifted loop through the back.

STITCH PATTERN
FIR CONE LACE
Rows 1, 3, 5 and 7 (RS): K1, yo, k3, sl 1, k2tog, psso, *k3, yo, k1, yo, k3, sl 1, k2tog, psso, repeat from * to last 4 stitches, k3, yo, k1.
Row 2 and all WS rows through 16: Purl.
Rows 9, 11, 13, and 15: K2tog, k3, yo, k1, *yo, k3, sl 1, k2tog, psso, k3, yo, k1, repeat from * to last 5 stitches, yo, k3, ssk. Repeat Rows 1–16 for pattern.

Sleeves (make 2)
Using double-pointed needles, cast on 30 (33, 36, 39, 42) stitches. Join, being careful not to twist. Place marker or use the tail of the yarn to mark the beginning of the round.
Round 1: *K1, p1; rep from * to end of the round, ending with k1 if needed.
Round 2: Purl the knit stitches and knit the purl stitches around.
Continue in stockinette stitch until sleeve measures 7 (7½, 8, 8½, 9)" [18(19, 20.5, 21.5, 23)cm] from beginning. On next round, remove marker, bind off 6 stitches, and place remaining stitches on a piece of scrap yarn. Set aside.

Skirt
Using larger needles, cast on 115 (125, 145, 155, 165) stitches. Knit 1 row (WS).
Next row (RS): K2, work Row 1 of Fir Cone Lace chart, end k2.
Next row (WS): Purl. Continue as established, working the first and last 2 stitches of each right-side row in stockinette.

Work in pattern until piece measures 15 (17, 19, 21, 23)" [38(43, 48.5, 53.5, 58.5)cm] from beginning.

Set-up row for decreases: K22 (25, 28, 31, 34), place marker, k71 (75, 89, 93, 97), place marker, k22 (25, 28, 31, 34). Purl next row.

Knit to marker, k9 (13, 12, 16, 20), [k2tog] 13 (12, 16, 15, 14) times, k1, [ssk] 13 (12, 16, 15, 14) times, k9 (13, 12, 16, 20), slip marker, knit to end–89 (101, 113, 125, 137) stitches remain.

Next row: Purl, decreasing 1 stitch at center back. Bind off all stitches on next right side row, do not break yarn. With wrong side facing, pick up 88 (100, 112, 124, 136) stitches to form a visible welt on the right side.

UPPER BODICE

Work in stockinette stitch for 1 (1½, 2, 2½, 3)" [2.5(3.8, 5, 6.5, 7.5)cm]. On next wrong-side row, p19 (22, 25, 28, 31), bind off 6 stitches purlwise, p38 (44, 50, 56, 62) stitches, bind off 6 stitches purlwise, purl to end.

Place held Sleeve stitches on a spare circular needle, or back onto double-pointed needles. On next row, knit to bound-off stitches, then knit across all held sleeve stitches, k38 (44, 50, 56, 62), attach second sleeve the same as first, knit to end–124 (142, 160, 178, 196) stitches.

Continue to work in stockinette stitch until work measures 5 (5½, 6, 6½, 7)" [12.5(14, 15, 16.5, 18)cm] from welt.

Decrease row 1 (RS): [K3, k2tog] across, end k4 (2, 0, 3, 1)–100 (114, 128, 143, 157) stitches. Work in stockinette stitch for 2", ending with a wrong side row.

Decrease row 2: [K2, k2tog]

across, end k0 (2, 0, 3, 1)–75 (86, 96, 108, 118) stitches. Work in stockinette stitch for 1½", ending with a wrong side row.

Decrease row 3: [K1, k2tog] across, end k0 (2, 0, 0, 1)–50 (58, 64, 72, 79) stitches. Work in stockinette stitch for 1½", ending with a wrong side row.

Decrease row 4: Decrease 11 (13,

14, 17, 18) stitches evenly across–39 (45, 50, 55, 61) stitches remain.
Next row: Bind off all stitches purlwise. Do not break yarn.

Hood

Using the same working yarn from the bound-off upper bodice stitches and with right side facing, pick up 39 (45, 50, 55, 61) stitches. Purl the next row.
Set-up row for increases: K13 (15, 17, 19, 20), place marker, k13 (15, 16, 17, 21), place marker, k13 (15, 17, 19, 20). Purl the next row.
Row 1 (RS): Knit to marker, M1R, slip marker, knit to next marker, slip marker, M1L, knit to end.
Row 2: Purl.
Repeat these 2 rows 10 times [59 (65, 70, 75, 81) stitches]. Work in stockinette stitch for 2" [5cm].
Begin decreases:
Row 1 (RS): Knit to 2 stitches before marker, k2tog, knit to next marker, ssk, knit to end.
Row 2: Purl.
Repeat these 2 rows 10 times–39 (45, 50, 55, 61) stitches remain.
Bind off all stitches on a right-side row. Fold the hood in half with wrong sides together and sew the seam.

Front Band

Using double-pointed needles, cast on 13 stitches.
Next row (RS): Slip 1 knitwise, [k1, p1] 5 times, end k2.

Next row (WS): P2, [k1, p1] 5 times, end k1. Repeat these 2 rows until the piece is approximately the same length as the entire front edge of the sweater (including hood). Leave stitches on the needle. With right sides facing, stretch the band slightly and sew it to the front edge of the body, beginning at the lower left edge. Continue until the entire edge is sewn on, adjusting the length of the band by knitting or ripping back rows if necessary. When the band is completely attached, bind off all band stitches.

Finishing

Sew the bound-off underarm stitches together. Weave in ends. Block the sweater to the finished measurements, paying special attention to the lace pattern on the skirt.
Make 4 button loops: Crochet a chain 5" [12.5cm] long for each. Sew the loops between the bodice and the front band evenly spaced along the right upper bodice. Sew the buttons opposite the button loops.

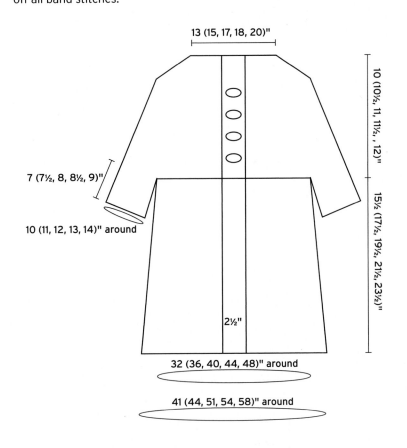

13 (15, 17, 18, 20)"

10 (10½, 11, 11½, 12)"

15½ (17½, 19½, 21½, 23½)"

7 (7½, 8, 8½, 9)"

10 (11, 12, 13, 14)" around

2½"

32 (36, 40, 44, 48)" around

41 (44, 51, 54, 58)" around

Fir Cone Lace Chart

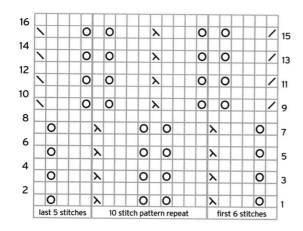

	K on right side, P on wrong side	
	Yarn over	O
	Slip 1 stitch, K2tog, psso	⋏
	K2tog	/
	SSK	\

3

VAMPIRE STYLE

Vampires don't have to worry about wrinkles, since they never age physically, but a vampire will want to develop her or his own sense of style. What do modern vampires wear? Tuxedos? Black capes? While these are classic looks, the vampires in modern tales have developed a more chic and up-to-date approach to fashion. Whether they sparkle in the sunlight or drink synthetic blood, the vampires of today are stylish and sexy.

Should you find yourself turned, or if you'd just like to emulate a vamp, the knits in this chapter are sure to keep you looking the part. Maybe it's something in a traditional black, like a delicate shrug or lacy scarf. Perhaps it's a pair of stockings knit in a deep red to remind you of the blood you crave. Your smoldering new wardrobe should at least include a sexy corset or a sleek capelet. There is even something for the littlest vamps.

Countess Bathory Scarf

Countess Elizabeth Bathory of Hungary became known as the "Blood Countess." She was accused of torturing and killing hundreds of young women and bathing in their blood, supposedly to preserve her own youth and beauty.

DESIGNED BY → Rilana Riley-Munson   SKILL LEVEL → Intermediate

SIZES
One size

FINISHED MEASUREMENTS
5½" x 44" (14cm x 112cm)

MATERIALS
Bernat Satin Sport (3) light (100% acrylic; 3 oz/85g, 221 yd/202m): 1 skein in 03430 Wine → Size 6 (4mm) straight needles → Stitch holders → Tapestry needle

GAUGE
26 stitches and 28 rows = 4" (10cm) in Feather and Fan pattern

SPECIAL SKILLS
→ **Kitchener stitch (page 137)**

STITCH PATTERNS
SEED STITCH
Row 1 (RS): *K1, p1; repeat from * to end.
Row 2: *P1, k1; repeat from * to end.
Repeat Rows 1 and 2 for pattern.

FEATHER AND FAN
Row 1 (RS): Knit.
Row 2: Purl.
Row 3: *[K2tog] 3 times, [yo, k1] 6 times, [k2tog] 3 times; repeat from * to end.
Row 4: Knit.
Repeat Rows 1-4 for pattern.

Scarf Half (make 2)
Cast on 36 stitches. Work in garter stitch (knit every row) for 4 rows. Change to Feather and Fan pattern and work even until piece measures 10½" (27cm) from start of lace pattern, ending with a wrong side row.
Next row (RS): *K2tog; repeat from * to end−18 sts.
Work in seed stitch for 10½" (27cm). Place stitches on holder and set aside.

Finishing
Graft the two halves of the scarf together using Kitchener stitch. Weave in ends.

· TID-BITE ·

In MOONLIGHT, a short-lived show in 2007, a private investigator/vampire Mick St. John, who was bitten by his vampire bride on their wedding night, now struggles with his love for a mortal woman.

Palm Readers

Now any human can be warm and cozy and as clairvoyant as a vamp when wearing these stylish wrist warmers, just like Alice Cullen was in the movie NEW MOON.

DESIGNED BY → Nancy Fry   SKILL LEVEL → Intermediate

SIZE
One size fits most

FINISHED MEASUREMENTS
7½" circumference x 10" long (19cm x 25cm)

MATERIALS
KnitPicks Bare Superwash Merino Worsted (4) medium (100% superwash wool; 3½ oz/100g, 220 yd/201m): 1 skein in Natural, dyed blue, aqua, and brown → Set of 4 size 7 (4.5mm) and 8 (5mm) double-pointed needles → Stitch markers → Tapestry needle

GAUGE
16 stitches and 24 rows = 4" (10cm) in stockinette stitch using larger needles

SPECIAL INSTRUCTIONS
→ **M1R:** From the back, lift loop between stitches with the left needle, knit into front of loop.
→ **M1L:** From the front, lift loop between stitches with the left needle, knit into back of loop.

Mitt (make 2)
With larger needles, cast on 30 stitches. Divide evenly over 3 needles and join in the round.
Work in k3, p2 rib for 2" (5cm). Work even in stockinette stitch for 3" (8cm) more or to desired length.

THUMB
Round 1: K15, pm, M1R, k1, M1L, pm, k14–32 sts.
Rounds 2 and 3: Knit.
Round 4: K15, sm, M1R, k3, M1L, sm, k14–34 sts.
Rounds 5 and 6: Knit.
Round 7: K15, sm, M1R, k5, M1L, sm, k14–36 sts.
Rounds 8 and 9: Knit.
Round 10: K15, sm, M1R, k7, M1L, sm, k14–38 sts.
Rounds 11 and 12: Knit.
Round 13: K15, sm, M1R, k9, M1L, sm, k14–40 sts.
Rounds 14 and 15: Knit.
Round 16: K15, sm, M1R, k11, M1L, sm, k14–42 sts.
Round 17: K15, bind off the 13 sts between markers, remove markers, cast on 1 st over gap, k14–30 sts.
Change to smaller needles. Work in k3, p2 rib for 2" (5cm). Bind off in pattern.

Finishing
Weave in ends.

Sitio Stockings

SITIO is Latin for "I'm thirsty," and whether you thirst for blood or not, these long stockings are beautiful, and not too hard to make—even for a beginning sock knitter.

DESIGNED BY → Ashley Fay  SKILL LEVEL → Easy

SIZE
Woman's S/M (M/L)

FINISHED MEASUREMENTS
7½ (8)" [19(20)cm] foot circumference
9½ (11)" [24(28)cm] calf circumference, unstretched

MATERIALS
KnitPicks Stroll Sock Yarn [1] super fine (75% superwash merino, 25% nylon; 1¾ oz/50 g, 231 yd/211m): 2 skeins in Firecracker Heather OR 500 yards of any sock weight yarn → Set of 5 size 1½ (2.5mm) double-pointed needles → Tapestry needle

GAUGE
32 stitches and 52 rows = 4" (10cm) in stockinette stitch

SPECIAL SKILLS
→ **Short rows (page 135)**
→ **Wrap and turn (W&T) (page 136)**
→ **Unwrap (UW) (page 136)**

SPECIAL INSTRUCTIONS
→ **Figure 8 cast-on:** Hold two double-pointed needles parallel in your left hand. Place the yarn tail between the two needles, with the tail facing you. Wrap the working yarns over the top needle, from back to front, then through the middle of the two needles, and under the bottom needle from back to front, and back through the middle. Continue wrapping the yarn in this figure-8 motion until you have half the specified stitches wrapped on one needle, and half on the other, with the wraps on both needles totaling the number of specified stitches. Using a third double-pointed needle, knit the stitches on the top needle, turn the needles 180 degrees and knit the stitches on the second needle. Distribute the stitches onto four double-pointed needles and continue working in the round according to the sock toe instructions.

→ **Sewn bind-off:** Thread a length of yarn three times the width of the bound off edge onto a tapestry needle. Working from right to left, insert the tapestry needle purlwise (right to left) through the first two stitches and pull the yarn through. Then bring the needle knitwise (left to right) through the first stitch. Pull the yarn through and drop the stitch off the knitting needle. Repeat until all stitches have been bound off.

NOTE
The stockings are knit from the toe up.

· TID-BITE ·
Selene from UNDERWORLD is both a vampire and a warrior fighting against the Lycans (werewolves), only to find herself falling in love with one.

Stocking (make 2)

TOE

Using a Figure 8 cast on, cast on 12 stitches on each of two needles, Needle 1 and Needle 2—24 stitches.

Round 1: Knit.

Round 2: K1, M1, knit to last stitch, M1, k1 on Needle 1; repeat on Needle 2.

Repeat Rounds 1 and 2 until there are 60 (64) stitches. Rearrange stitches onto 4 needles, 15 (16) stitches on each needle; instep stitches on Needles 1 and 2, sole stitches on Needles 3 and 4. Knit 4 (2) rounds even.

INSTEP

Round 1: K2, *ssk, yo; repeat from * to 2 stitches before end of Needle 2, k2. Knit all stitches on Needles 3 and 4.

Round 2: Knit.

Repeat Rounds 1 and 2 until foot reaches your ankle bone, ending with Row 2 and Needle 2.

HEEL

Row 1 (RS): Knit to last stitch, W&T.

Row 2: Purl to last stitch, W&T.

Row 3: Knit to 1 stitch before last wrapped stitch, W&T.

Row 4: Purl to 1 stitch before last wrapped stitch, W&T.

Continue as established until there are 10 wrapped stitches on each side.

Row 1 (RS): Knit to first wrapped stitch, UW, W&T.

Row 2: Purl to first wrapped stitch, UW, W&T.

Row 3: Knit to next wrapped stitch, UW, W&T.

Row 4: Purl to next wrapped stitch, UW, W&T.

Continue until all stitches are unwrapped. Resume working in the round.

LEG

Round 1: *Ssk, yo; repeat from * to end of round.

Round 2: Knit.

Repeat Rounds 1 and 2 until stocking reaches the base of your calf muscle, ending with Round 2.

INCREASE

* Round 1: Work as for Round 1, M1.

Round 2: Work as for Round 2, M1 (2 stitches increased).

Work even in pattern for 11 rounds.

Repeat from * until there are 76 (88) stitches.

Continue working even in pattern until stocking reaches your thigh.

Next round: *K1, p1; repeat from * to end of round. Work even for 1" (2.5cm). Bind off loosely (sewn bind-off recommended).

Finishing

Weave in ends. Block.

The Prim Reaper's Corset

For her costumes and her charming creepiness, Drusilla, the prim reaper, was always my favorite Buffy baddie. I coveted her clothing; even her underwear was fetching. This waist corset was inspired by the sweet nothings she wore in "Destiny" (ANGEL Season 5), but it is worked in a rich, Victorian color scheme to make it equally striking as outerwear.

DESIGNED BY ⇥ Nikol Lohr　　SKILL LEVEL ⇥ Experienced

SIZE
Women's S (M, L, XL)

FINISHED MEASUREMENTS
To fit waist size 24-26 (27-32, 33-36, 37-40)" [61-66 (69-81, 84-91, 94-102) cm]

NOTE
Adjust up or down to fit by choosing the closest size and working fewer or more Linen Stitch rows in each panel.

MATERIALS
Louet MerLin Sport (3) light (60% linen, 40% merino wool; 3½ oz/100g, 250 yd/228m): 1 (2, 2, 3) skeins in Pewter [MC] ⇥ Louet MerLin Sport (3) light (60% linen, 40% merino wool; 3½ oz/100g, 250 yd/228m): 1 skein each Caribou [CC1] and Linen Gray [CC2] ⇥ Sizes 3 (3.25mm) and 7 (4.5mm) circular knitting needles ⇥ Size E (3.5mm) crochet hook ⇥ 4 yd (4m) ⅜" ribbon (shown: Offray center stitch ribbon) ⇥ 2 yd (2m) twill-covered boning (available at fabric stores) ⇥ Blunt and sharp yarn needles ⇥ Sewing needle and matching thread

GAUGE
21 stitches = 4" (10cm) with 2 strands held together in stockinette stitch on smaller needles
22 stitches = 4" (10cm) with 2 strands held together in Linen stitch on larger needles

SPECIAL SKILLS
⇥ **Short rows (page 135)**

SPECIAL INSTRUCTIONS
⇥ **S1WYIF:** With yarn held to front of work, slip 1 stitch.

⇥ **S1WYIB:** With yarn held to back of work, slip 1 stitch.

STITCH PATTERN
LINEN STITCH
Row 1 (RS): *K1, S1WYIF; repeat from * across.
Row 2: *P1, S1WYIB; repeat from * across.
Repeat Rows 1 and 2 for pattern, making sure to knit (or purl) in previous row's slipped stitches, and slip stitches that were knit (or purled) on previous row.

NOTES
Use two strands of yarn held together for the entire corset body and a single strand for the top and bottom edging. For ease, wind all yarn into center-pull balls and use both ends.
Maintain a slipped-stitch edge throughout: Always slip the first stitch and knit the last stitch. On short rows, maintain the slipped-stitch edge and work the turns in pattern.

· TID-BITE ·
Drusilla from BUFFY THE VAMPIRE SLAYER was turned into a vampire by Angelus (called Angel after he regained his soul) on the day she was to take her vows as a nun. She possesses psychic abilities and uses them to her advantage.

Corset

LACE-UP EYELET EDGING

Provisional Cast-on: With CC2 and crochet hook, loosely chain 45 (45, 51, 57).

With CC1 and smaller needles, and leaving a 24" (61cm) tail, pick up and knit 45 (45, 51, 57) stitches, one through the underside bump of each crocheted chain. (Later, you'll unravel the CC2 yarn and have live stitches to tack down around the boning.)

Beginning with a wrong side row, work 4 rows in stockinette stitch. Work 1 row in reverse stockinette. Work 4 rows in stockinette. Change to larger needles. Slip 1 and bind off across the row, leaving 1 live stitch at the end of the row. With smaller needles, pick up 44 (44, 50, 56) stitches.

Next row (RS): Change to CC2. Sl 1, knit to end.

Next row (WS): Slip 1, purl to 1 stitch from end, k1.

Next row (RS): Slip 1, *yo, k2tog; repeat from * to the end of the row.

Next row (WS): Slip 1, purl to 1 stitch from end, k1.

Next row (RS): Change to CC1 and larger needles. Slip 1 and bind off across row, leaving 1 live stitch at the end.

Next row (WS): Change to smaller needles. Slip 1, pick up 44 (44, 50, 56) stitches.

Back Panel 1

Next row (RS): Change to MC and larger needles. Begin Linen Stitch:

Slip 1, *S1WYIF, k1; repeat from * across.

Next row (WS): Slip 1, *p1, S1WYIB; repeat from * to 1 stitch from end, k1.

Decrease along bottom edge:

Next row (RS): Slip 1, ssk, work in pattern to end.

Work wrong side row in pattern. Continue working decreases every right side row until 39 (39, 43, 49) stitches remain. Work wrong side row in pattern.

Shape upper flare of back panel:

Next row (RS): Slip 1, work in pattern to end.

Size XL only:

Next row (WS): Slip 1, work 13 stitches in pattern, wrap and turn.

Next row (RS): Work in pattern back to top edge.

All sizes:

Next row (WS): Slip 1, work 19 stitches in pattern, wrap and turn.

Next row (RS): Work in pattern back to top edge.

Next row (WS): Slip 1, work 23 stitches in pattern, wrap and turn.

Next row (RS): Work in pattern back to top edge.

Next row (WS): Slip 1, work 19 stitches in pattern, wrap and turn.

Next row (RS): Work in pattern back to top edge.

Sizes L & XL only:

Next row (WS): Slip 1, work 13 stitches in pattern, wrap and turn.

Next row (RS): Work in pattern back to top edge.

· CORSET CONSTRUCTION ·

The corset is knit side-to-side with two strands of yarn that results in a strong fabric with a soft hand and fluid drape. It is knit at a tight tension for a fairly firm fabric, and then further enforced with twill-covered boning sewn inside for support.

The corset is comprised of five panels (two lacing panels, two side panels, one front panel) delineated by bound-off stitches, then picked-up "boning," which will later conceal the sewn-in boning. Starting at the lacing, each panel is worked, then bound off and picked up repeatedly to make the boning sections. You'll bind off with larger needles and pick up with the smaller ones, using a crochet hook to help with tight stitches. You'll also use the larger needles for the Linen Stitch and the smaller needles for everything else. The three-dimensional hip shaping is created with intense short rows in the side panels, with less dramatic short rows in the other direction to taper the front and back panels.

All sizes:

Next row (WS): Slip 1, work in pattern to 1 stitch from edge, k1.

Boning Between Panels

Next row (RS): Change to smaller needles. Slip 1, knit through back loop of all stitches (to twist the stitches and firm up the work before the boning).

Without turning the work, begin another right side row:

Next row (RS): With CC1 and larger needles, slip 1, then bind off that and all stitches to the end, leaving 1 live stitch.

Next row (WS): Change to smaller needles. Pick up and knit 38 (38, 42, 48) stitches.

Change to MC and repeat the last two rows.

Change to CC1 and larger needles and work the first row of the set.

Change to MC and smaller needles and work the second row of set.

Side Panel

Change to larger needles. Maintaining slipped-stitch edge, work a total of 6 (10, 12, 14) rows in Linen Stitch.

SHORT ROW HIP SHAPING

Size XL only:

Next row (RS): Slip 1, work 12 stitches in pattern, wrap and turn.

Next row (WS): Work in pattern to bottom edge.

All sizes:

Next row (RS): Slip 1, work 16 stitches in pattern, wrap and turn.

Next row (WS): Work in pattern to bottom edge.

Next row (RS): Slip 1, work 20 stitches in pattern, wrap and turn.

Next row (WS): Work in pattern to bottom edge.

Next row (RS): Slip 1, work 24 stitches in pattern, wrap and turn.

Next row (WS): Work in pattern to bottom edge.

Next row (RS): Slip 1, work 20 stitches in pattern, wrap and turn.

Next row (WS): Work in pattern to bottom edge.

Next row (RS): Slip 1, work 16 stitches in pattern, wrap and turn.

Next row (WS): Work in pattern to bottom edge.

Sizes L and XL only:

Next row (RS): Slip 1, work 12 stitches in pattern, wrap and turn.

Next row (WS): Work in pattern to bottom edge.

All sizes:

Work for a total of 6 (10, 12, 14) rows in pattern.

Repeat entire Short Row Hip Shaping section a total of 3 (3, 4, 4) times.

If you have a small waist for your hip size, you may reduce the number of full rows between short rows and add an extra repeat or two here for more dramatic hip shaping.

Repeat BONING section.

Front Panel

With larger needles, maintaining slipped-stitch edge, work 2 rows in Linen Stitch.

Begin increases:

Next row (RS): Slip 1, M1, work in pattern to end.

Work WS row in pattern.

Continue increase every RS row until you have 45 (45, 51, 57) stitches. Work next wrong side row in pattern.

EYELET TRIM

Next row (RS): Change to smaller needles. Slip 1, knit through back loop of all stitches.

Without turning work, begin another right side row:

Next row (RS): Change to CC2 and larger needles. Slip 1, then bind off that and all stitches to the end, leaving 1 live stitch.

Next row (WS): Change to smaller needles. Pick up and knit 44 (44, 50, 56) stitches.

Next row (RS): Slip 1, *yo, k2tog; repeat from * to end of row.

Next row (WS): Slip 1, purl to one stitch from end of row, k1.

Next row (RS): Change to larger needles. Slip 1, then bind off that and all stitches to the end, leaving 1 live stitch.

Next row (WS): Change to smaller needles. Pick up and knit 44 (44, 50, 56) stitches.

Next row (RS): Change to CC1 and larger needles. Slip 1, then bind off that and all stitches to the end, leaving one live stitch.

Next row (WS): Change to smaller needles. Pick up and knit 44 (44, 50, 56) stitches.

CHECKERS

Next row (RS): Change to CC2 and larger needles. Begin Linen stitch: Slip 1, *S1WYIF, k1; repeat from * to end.

Next row (WS): Slip 1, work in pattern to one stitch from end, k1. Change to CC1 and repeat last 2 rows.

Work all 4 rows 1 (3, 4, 5) times more.

FLARE TOP OF CENTER PLACKET

Next row (RS): Change to CC2. Work in pattern to end.

Size XL only:

Next row (WS): Slip 1, work 7 stitches in pattern, wrap and turn.

Next row (RS): Work in pattern back to top edge.

All sizes:

Next row (WS): Slip 1, work 13 stitches in pattern, wrap and turn.

Next row (RS): Work in pattern back to top edge.

Next row (WS): Slip 1, work 19 stitches in pattern, wrap and turn.

Next row (RS): Work in pattern back to top edge.

Next row (WS): Slip 1, work 25 stitches in pattern, wrap and turn.

Next row (RS): Work in pattern back to top edge.

Next row (WS): Slip 1, work 19 stitches in pattern, wrap and turn.

Next row (RS): Work in pattern back to top edge.

Next row (WS): Slip 1, work 13 stitches in pattern, wrap and turn.

Next row (RS): Work in pattern back to top edge.

Sizes L & XL only:

Next row (WS): Slip 1, work 7 stitches in pattern, wrap and turn.

Next row (RS): Work in pattern back to top edge.

All Sizes:

Next row (WS): Work row in pattern.

RESUME CHECKERS

Next row (RS): Change to CC1 and larger needles. Begin Linen stitch: Slip 1, *S1WYIF, k1; repeat from * to end.

Next row (WS): Slip 1, work in pattern to 1 stitch from end, k1. Change to CC1 and repeat last 2 rows.

Work all 4 rows 1 (3, 4, 5) times more.

EYELET TRIM

Next row (RS): Change to smaller needles. Knit through back loop across row.

Next row (RS): Without turning work, change to CC1 and larger needles. Slip 1, then bind off that and all stitches to the end, leaving one live stitch.

Next row (WS): Change to smaller needles. Pick up and knit 44 (44, 50, 56) stitches.

Next row (RS): Change to larger needles and CC2. Slip 1, then bind off that and all stitches to the end, leaving 1 live stitch.

Next row (WS): Change to smaller needles. Pick up and knit 44 (44, 50, 56) stitches.

Next row (RS): Slip 1, *yo, k2tog; repeat from * to end of row.

Next row (WS): Slip 1, purl to one stitch from end of row, k1.

Next row (RS): Change to larger needles. Slip 1, then bind off that and all stitches to the end, leaving one live stitch.

Next row (WS): Change to smaller needles. Pick up and knit 44 (44, 50, 56) stitches.

Change to MC. Work 2 rows in Linen Stitch.

BEGIN DECREASE

Next row (RS): Slip 1, ssk, work in pattern to the end.

Work WS row in pattern.

Continue working decreases every right side row until 39 (39, 43, 49) stitches remain. Work wrong side row in pattern.

Work 2 more rows in pattern.

Repeat BONING section.
Repeat SIDE PANEL section.
Repeat BONING section.

Back Panel 2

Change to larger needles.

SHAPE UPPER FLARE OF BACK PANEL

Next row (RS): Slip 1, work in pattern to end.

Size XL only:

Next row (WS): Slip 1, work 13 stitches in pattern, wrap and turn.

Next row (RS): Work in pattern back to top edge.

All sizes:

Next row (WS): Slip 1, work 19 stitches in pattern, wrap and turn.

Next row (RS): Work in pattern back to top edge.

Next row (WS): Slip 1, work 23 stitches in pattern, wrap and turn.

Next row (RS): Work in pattern back to top edge.

Next row (WS): Slip 1, work 19 stitches in pattern, wrap and turn.

Next row (RS): Work in pattern back to top edge.

Sizes L and XL only:

Next row (WS): Slip 1, work 13 stitches in pattern, wrap and turn.

Next row (RS): Work in pattern back to top edge.

All sizes:

Next row (WS): Slip 1, work in pattern to 1 stitch from edge, k1.

Increase along bottom edge

Next row (RS): Slip 1, M1, work in pattern to end.

Work wrong side row in pattern. Continue working increases every right side row until 45 (45, 51, 57) stitches remain. Work wrong side row in pattern.

Next row (RS): Work in pattern.

Next row (WS): Slip 1, purl through back loop to last stitch, k1.

LACE-UP EYELET EDGING

Change to CC1 and large needles. Slip 1, bind off across row, leaving one live stitch at end.

Change to smaller needles and pick up and knit 44 (44, 50, 56) stitches.

Next row (RS): Change to CC2. Sl 1, knit to end.

Next row (WS): Slip 1, purl to one stitch from end, k1.

Next row (RS): Slip 1, *yo, k2tog; repeat from * to end of row.

Next row (WS): Slip 1, purl to one stitch from end, k1.

Next row (RS): Change to CC1 and larger needles. Slip 1 and bind off across row, leaving one live stitch at the end.

Next row (WS): Change to smaller needles. Slip 1, pick up and knit 44 (44, 50, 56) stitches.

Work 4 rows in stockinette stitch, ending with a right side row.

Work one row in reverse stockinette.

Work 4 rows in stockinette, ending with a wrong side row.

Transfer all stitches to a strand of CC2 yarn to hold, leaving a 24" (61cm) tail for sewing down live stitches.

Finishing

BLOCK

Using a sharp yarn needle, weave in all ends except the long tails at either end, weaving the ends through the back of the boning sections to keep the panel fabric smooth. You can leave a longer than usual tail if you like, because it will be concealed under the sewn-in boning.

Soak the corset in hot water, press out excess water, and block to straighten the edges and points, flatten the eyelet, straighten boning sections, and eliminate bias.

PREPARE BONING

Cut 2 lengths of boning 1½" (4cm) longer than lace-up edge.

Cut 4 lengths of boning 1½" (4cm) longer than boning stitch sections. Slide the boning partially out of twill casing on one end, and snip off 1½" (4cm) from each piece. Slide boning back down to the center of the casing.

Fold over each edge of twill casing twice and tack down with needle and thread (creating a hem on either side).

Lightly steam press the boning if necessary to flatten it. (Boning can retain the curve from the roll.)

MAKE CASING FOR BONING ON BACK EDGE

Unravel the last stitch of the crochet chain from the provisional cast-on. After the stitch is open, you should be able to gently pull on the chain and unravel it easily,

transferring each live cast-on stitch to waste yarn. (The end of the crochet chain threaded onto a yarn needle works well.)

With wrong side facing, place the longer boning piece on the stockinette edge and fold at the reverse stockinette row to enclose the boning. Using the reserved yarn tail and a blunt yarn needle, tack down the stockinettte stitch, drawing the strand through a CC1 purl bump along the outside edge of the eyelet, then through one live stitch until all live stitches have been secured. Tack down the end and draw it through the casing so the tail is left hidden in casing. Repeat on the other side.

TRIM TOP AND BOTTOM

Use one strand of yarn for the trim.

With right side facing, CC1, and smaller needles, pick up and knit one stitch along each slipped-stitch edge stitch (i.e., one stitch for every 2 rows of the corset), working from the CC2 lacing eyelet to the lacing eyelet (skip the stockinette casing). Turn work. Slip 1 and knit across row, then pick up and knit one stitch through both layers of the top of the stockinette casing. Turn work and bind off to last stitch, then pick up and knit one stitch through both layers of the top of the stockinette casing and bind off remainder of row. Use the two ends and a sharp yarn needle to sew up the open ends of the stockinette casing, then draw them through the casing, penetrating the twill inside. Be sure to conceal any stitches within the knitting.

Repeat along bottom edge.

SEW IN BONING

Working from the wrong side, using a sewing needle and thread and a whipstitch, carefully sew the prepared boning strips along the boning stitches, working into the purl bumps. Position the prepared boning strips so that the folded/hemmed ends are facing the knitting and the smooth side faces the body.

Block again if necessary, or steam press.

LACING

Use every other eyelet to lace the corset with ribbon. Start with the ends coming from the inside of the corset toward the outside. Cross them on the top side of the work, then feed them back into the second eyelets down on the opposite sides. Then cross them on the underside (toward the body), feed them back out from the inside, cross again on the outside, and so forth, alternating from front to back as shown. After the corset is laced, tighten the ribbon section by section, and tie the ends in a bow at the bottom.

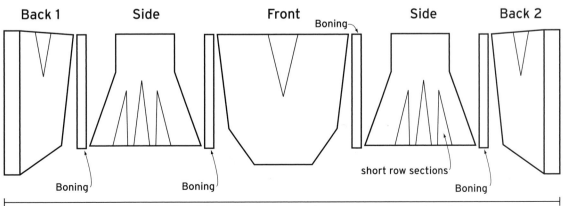

Aprox. 22 (24, 30, 36)", measured across narrowest point

Be Still My Beating Heart Capelet

Modern vampire girls don't have to hide under long cumbersome cloaks. Instead, they can wear this delicate capelet with a hood.

DESIGNED BY → Ashley Fay   SKILL LEVEL → Intermediate

SIZE
Women's S (M, L, XL)

FINISHED MEASUREMENTS
To fit bust: 32 (34, 36, 38)" [81 (86, 91, 97)cm]

MATERIALS
skeins KnitPicks Gloss Fingering (1) super fine (70% merino wool, 30% silk; 1¾ oz/50g, 220 yd/201m): 3(4, 4, 5) in Dusk → Size 3 (3.25mm) circular → 2 double-pointed needles → Stitch markers → Tapestry needle → 1 small button

GAUGE
27 stitches and 32 rows = 4" (10cm) in stockinette stitch

SPECIAL SKILLS
→ **Cables (page 134)**
→ **3-Needle bind-off (page 135)**
→ **I-cord (page 137)**

SPECIAL INSTRUCTIONS
→ **I-Cord bind-off:** Cast on 3 stitches using a double-pointed needle, *k2, k2tog, slide these 3 stitches back to the right end of the double-pointed needle; repeat from * until all stitches have been bound off.

→ **Applied I-Cord:** Pick up stitches along all of the edges, one stitch for every stitch on the bottom edge, and 3 stitches for every 4 rows on the sides of the piece. Cast on 3 stitches (for the regular capelet, there will already be 3 stitches from the I-cord bind-off), *k2, k2tog, slide these 3 stitches back to the right end of the double-pointed needle; repeat from * until the I-cord is complete on all sides of the capelet.

NOTE
This pattern has eight decrease points that are separated by two stitches. You decrease on either side of these two stitches and, at the same time, work one repeat of the Heart chart. After the chart is complete, continue making the 8-point decreases as established.

Capelet
Cast on 349 (365, 381, 397) stitches.
Row 1 (WS): P50 (52, 54, 56), pm, p2, pm, p67 (71, 75, 79), pm, p2, pm, p107 (111, 115, 119), pm, p2, pm, p67(71, 75, 79), pm, p2, pm, p50 (52, 54, 56).
Row 2: Knit.
Row 3: Purl.
Row 4: K5, pm, work Row 1 of Heart chart (page 75) over next 15 stitches, pm, k5, pm, work Row 1 of chart, pm, knit to 2 sts before marker, k2tog, sm, k2, sm, k2tog, k3(5, 7, 9), pm, *work Row 1 of chart, pm, k5, pm; repeat from * once more, work Row 1 of chart, pm, knit to 2 stitches before marker, ssk, sm, k2, sm, k2tog, k7(9, 11, 13), pm, **work Row 1 of chart,

pm, k5, pm; repeat from ** 3 times more, work Row 1 of chart, pm, knit to 2 stitches before marker, ssk, sm, k2, sm, k2tog, k3(5, 7, 9), pm, ***work Row 1 of chart, pm, k5, pm; repeat from *** once more, work Row 1 of chart, pm, knit to 2 stitches before marker, ssk, sm, k2, sm, k2tog, k8(10, 12, 14), pm, work Row 1 of chart, pm, k5, pm, work Row 1 of chart, pm, knit to end.

Row 5: Purl.

Row 6: Knit to marker, sm, work Row 3 of chart, sm, knit to marker, sm, work Row 3 of chart, sm, knit to marker, sm, k2, sm, knit to marker, sm, *work Row 3 of chart, sm, knit to marker, sm; repeat from * once more, work Row 3 of chart, sm, knit to marker, sm, k2, sm, knit to marker sm, **work Row 3 of chart, sm, knit to marker, sm; repeat from ** 3 times more, work Row 3 of chart, sm, knit to marker, sm, k2, sm, knit to marker, sm, ***work Row 3 of chart, sm, knit to marker, sm; repeat from *** once more, work Row 3 of chart, sm, knit to marker, sm, k2, sm, knit to marker, sm, work Row 3 of chart, sm, knit to marker, sm, work Row 3 of chart, sm, knit to end.

Row 7: Purl.

Row 8: *Knit to marker, sm, work Row 5 of chart, sm; repeat from * once more, knit to 2 stitches before marker, ssk, sm, k2, sm, k2tog, **knit to marker, sm, work Row 5 of chart, sm; repeat from

** twice more, knit to 2 stitches before marker, ssk, sm, k2, sm, k2tog, ***knit to marker, sm, work Row 5 of chart, sm; repeat from *** 4 times more, knit to 2 stitches before marker, ssk, sm, k2, sm, k2tog, ****knit to marker, sm, work Row 5 of chart, sm; repeat from **** twice more, knit to 2 stitches before marker, ssk, sm, k2, sm, k2tog, *****knit to marker, sm,

work Row 5 of chart, sm; repeat from ***** once more, knit to end.

Row 9: Purl.

Repeat Rows 6–9 until all rows of the Heart chart are complete. For the smaller sizes, you may need to decrease from the end stitches on the chart. Remove the markers from the chart repeats, but leave the stitch markers that mark the decrease points.

Row 1 (RS): *Knit to 2 stitches before marker, ssk, sm, k2, sm, k2tog; repeat from * 3 times more, knit to end.
Row 2: Purl.
Row 3: Knit.
Row 4: Purl.
Repeat these 4 rows until 109 (117, 125, 133) stitches remain, ending with a wrong-side row.

Hood

Next row (RS): Knit, decreasing one stitch in the middle of this row—108 (116, 124, 132) stitches.
Next row: Purl.
Work in stockinette stitch until hood measures 6" (15cm), ending with a wrong side row.
The rest of the hood will be worked in two halves. Divide stitches in half, 54 (58, 62, 66) stitches per side.

RIGHT HALF

Row 1 (RS): K53 (57, 61, 65), turn.
Row 2: Purl.
Row 3: K52 (56, 60, 64), turn.
Row 4: Purl back across these stitches.
Continue in this manner, working each right-side row 1 stitch shorter than the previous one, until there are 27 (29, 31, 33) stitches being worked. Turn and purl back. Break yarn, leaving a 6" (15cm) tail.
Place all 54 (58, 62, 66) Right Half stitches on a holder.
For the left half, begin on the wrong side.

LEFT HALF

Row 1 (WS): P53 (57, 61, 65), turn.
Row 2: Purl.
Row 3: K52 (56, 60, 64), turn.
Row 4: Purl.
Continue in this manner, working each wrong-side row 1 stitch shorter than the previous one, until there are 27 (29, 31, 33) stitches being worked. Turn and knit across. Leave all 54 (58, 62, 66) Left Half stitches on the needle.

Finishing

Place the Right Half of the stitches on another needle and hold the two needles parallel, right sides of the hood together, and join using a 3-needle bind-off.
Begin applied I-cord on the bottom edge of the capelet, continue up the side, to the beginning of the hood, knit regular I-cord for 4 rows (or more, depending on how large your button is), and continue with applied I-cord around the hood and on the other edge until all edges have been worked. Bind off. Weave in ends. Sew button opposite button loop.

Heart Chart

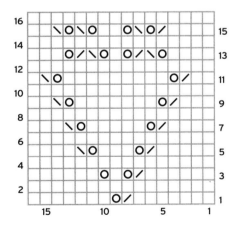

K on right side, P on wrong side
Yarn over
K2tog
SSK

The Black Veil

The Black Veil is a code of conduct set down by vampires and also represents the veil of secrecy that vampires live under. With the exception of a few modern vamps, most vampires live in secrecy and hide under cover of night.

DESIGNED BY → Kimberly Dijkstra   SKILL LEVEL → Intermediate

SIZE
One size

FINISHED MEASUREMENTS
6" x 78" (15cm x 198cm)

MATERIALS
Patons Silk Bamboo (3) light (70% bamboo, 30% silk; 2¼ oz /65g, 102 yd /93m): 2 skeins in 85040 Coal → Size 7 (4.5mm) straight needles → Tapestry needle

GAUGE
17 stitches and 24 rows = 4" (10cm)

SPECIAL INSTRUCTIONS
→ **Knitted cast-on:** Make a slipknot on left-hand needle, *knit 1 stitch and place it onto left-hand needle without dropping first stitch; repeat from *, always knitting into the last stitch made.

→ **Picot cast-on:** *Cast on 5 stitches with knitted cast on method, bind off 2 stitches, slip the stitch on right-hand needle to left-hand needle; repeat from * across.

→ **Picot bind-off:** *Cast on 2 stitches with knitted cast-on method, bind off 5 stitches, slip the stitch on right-hand needle to left-hand needle; repeat from * across.

Scarf
Work picot cast-on 8 times, cast on 1 stitch more–25 sts.

Row 1: Knit.

Rows 2 and 3: Cast on 2 stitches, bind off 2 stitches, k1, *yo, p3tog, yo, k3; repeat from * 3 times, yo, p3tog, yo, k2.

Rows 4 and 5: K2, *yo, p3tog, yo, k3; repeat from * 3 times, yo, p3tog, yo, k2.

Rows 6 and 7: Repeat Rows 2 and 3.

Rows 8 and 9: K2, *k3, yo, p3tog, yo; repeat from * 3 times, k5.

Rows 10 and 11: Cast on 2 stitches, bind off 2 stitches, k1, *k3, yo, p3tog, yo; repeat from * 3 times, k5.

Rows 12 and 13: Repeat Rows 8 and 9.

Repeat Rows 2–13 until piece measures 78" (198cm) or desired length, ending with Row 7.

Next row: Knit.

Work picot bind-off 8 times, fasten off.

Finishing
Weave in ends. Dampen and block, pinning each picot into place. Allow to dry completely.

Sidhe Lace Shrug

According to myth, the Irish Sidhe was a beautiful fairy that lured men to their deaths and fed on their blood. This delicate lace shrug is perfect for fairies and vamps alike.

DESIGNED BY → Ashley Fay   SKILL LEVEL → Intermediate

SIZE
Women's S (M, L, XL)

FINISHED MEASUREMENTS
Upper arm circumference: 10 (12, 12, 14)" [25 (30, 30, 36)cm]
Length from cuff to center back: 24½ (25, 25½, 26)" [62 (64, 65, 66)cm] or as desired

MATERIALS
KnitPicks Alpaca Cloud lace (100% baby alpaca; 1¾ oz/50g, 440 yd/400m): 2 (2, 3, 3) skeins in Midnight →Set of 4 size 3 (3.25mm) double-pointed needles → Stitch markers → Stitch holders → Tapestry needle

GAUGE
22 stitches and 30 rows = 4" (10cm) in pattern with yarn held double

SPECIAL SKILLS
→ Kitchener stitch (page 137)

Shrug Half (make 2)
SLEEVE
With yarn held double, cast on 33 (36, 40, 44) stitches using the long-tail cast-on. Place marker and join in the round, being careful not to twist the stitches.

Work Row 1 of Lace Pattern chart (page 80) over the first 33 (33, 33, 44) stitches, knit 0 (3, 7, 0) stitches.
Continue in this manner until you have completed 5 repeats of Lace Pattern chart (page 80).
Continue to work the Lace chart and, at the same time, begin increasing 1 stitch at the end of each round every 4 rounds 11 (8, 4, 11) times. Work increased stitches in stockinette stitch until there are enough for an additional repeat, then work those stitches in Lace pattern as well—44 (44, 44, 55) sts. Continue as established, increasing as before, until there are 55 (55, 66, 66) sts.
Sizes M and XL only: Continued as established, increasing as before, until there are 55 (66, 66, 77) sts.
All sizes: Work even until sleeve measures approximately 18" (46cm) or desired length to underarm, ending with Row 1 of chart. Turn work, and purl across all stitches.

BACK
Measure across your back from shoulder to shoulder, then divide this number in half (A). Work back and forth in rows in Lace Pattern for A" (Acm) or 6½ (7, 7½, 8)" [17(18, 19, 20) cm], ending with Row 8 of chart. Place stitches on a holder.

Finishing
Graft two halves together at center back using Kitchener stitch.
Weave in ends.
Block to finished measurements.

Lace Pattern

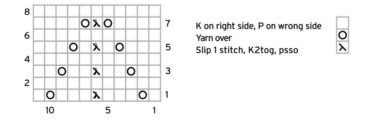

K on right side, P on wrong side
Yarn over
Slip 1 stitch, K2tog, psso

· WHO'S WHO ·
AMONG VAMPS

So much blood, so little time...
Test your knowledge of who's who among the denizens of the night.

1 Which one of these vampires drinks human blood with no qualms?

a) Edward Cullen from *Twilight*
b) Stefan Salvatore from *The Vampire Diaries*
c) Damon Salvatore from *The Vampire Diaries*
d) Emmett Cullen from *Twilight*

2 The bar that Eric Northman, from the Sookie Stackhouse series, owns in Shreveport, Louisiana is called:

a) The Fang Banger
b) Fangtasia
c) The Dark Knight
d) Bloodsucker

3 In the TWILIGHT series, which member of the Cullens never turned a human into a vampire?

a) Edward Cullen
b) Jasper Whitlock
c) Carlisle Cullen
d) Rosalie Hale

4 Which one of these vampires did not have mind-reading or psychic powers of any kind?

a) Alice Cullen from *Twilight*
b) Drusilla from *Buffy the Vampire Slayer*
c) Bill Compton from *True Blood* and the Sookie Stackhouse series
d) Edward Cullen from *Twilight*

5 Which one of these vampires has not had a human girlfriend?

a) Angel from *Buffy the Vampire Slayer*
b) Edward Cullen from *Twilight*
c) Stefan Salvatore from *The Vampire Diaries*
d) Jasper Hale from *Twilight*

6 Match the Vampire with his or her trait.

A Eric Northman
B Edward Cullen
C Spike
D Lestat de Lioncourt
E Alice Cullen
F Damon Salvatore

i. Was a poet as a human
ii. Was turned in an insane asylum
iii. Wears a ring that allows him to go out in the sunlight
iv. Was a Viking as a human
v. Was turned after almost dying of the Spanish flu
vi. Was an actor as a human

Little Fang Sweater

What's more emblematic of the dark side than a design based on a traditional yellow smiley face, but with a vampiric twist? Rather than a complete face, it has two fangs at the bottom of the sweater where the mouth would be.

DESIGNED BY → Tonya Wagner   SKILL LEVEL → Intermediate

SIZE
Children's 2 (3, 4, 5, 6) years

FINISHED MEASUREMENTS
Chest: 29 (30, 31, 32, 33)" [74 (76, 79, 81, 84)cm]

MATERIALS
KnitPicks Swish DK (3) light (100% superwash merino wool; 1¾ oz/50g, 123 yd/112m): 5 (5, 6, 6, 6) skeins in Cobblestone Heather [MC] → KnitPicks Swish DK (3) light (100% superwash merino wool; 1¾ oz/50g, 123 yd/112m): 1 skein each in Serrano [CC1] and White [CC2] → Size 5 (3.75mm) straight and 16" circular needles → Size 6 (4mm) straight needles → Bobbins (for intarsia) → Tapestry needle

GAUGE
24 stitches and 32 rows = 4" (10cm) in stockinette stitch using larger needles

SPECIAL SKILLS
→ **Stranded knitting (page 134)**

Back
With CC1 and smaller needles, cast on 81 (84, 87, 90, 93) stitches. Work in k1, p1 rib, ending with k1 if needed, for 1¼" (3cm), ending with a wrong side row.

Next row (RS): Increase 6 stitches evenly-spaced across row [87 (90, 93, 96, 99) stitches]. Change to MC and larger needles. Work in stockinette stitch until piece measures 9½ (10, 10½, 11, 11½)" [24 (25, 27, 28, 29)cm], ending with a wrong side row.

SHAPE ARMHOLES
Next (decrease) row (RS): K1, ssk, knit to last 3 stitches, k2tog, k1.

Work even in stockinette stitch for 3 (3, 3, 3, 1) rows.

Size 4 only: Work decrease row. Work 3 rows stockinette stitch.

All sizes: Repeat decrease row on next and every following right side row 20 (22, 22, 26, 27) times more–45 (44, 45, 42, 43) sts. Bind off remaining stitches for back neck.

Front
With CC1 and smaller needles, cast on 81 (84, 87, 90, 93) stitches. Work in k1, p1 rib, ending with k1 if needed, for 1¼" (3cm), ending with a wrong side row.

Next row (RS): Increase 6 stitches evenly spaced across row [87 (90, 93, 96, 99) stitches].

Change to MC and larger needles. Work in stockinette stitch until piece measures 3½" (9cm), ending with a wrong side row.

Next row (RS): K29 (31, 32, 34, 35) stitches, work Row 1 of chart (page 85), knit to end.

Continue as established, working chart until complete. Work even in stockinette stitch and MC until piece measures the same as the Back to armhole shaping.

SHAPE ARMHOLES

Next (decrease) row (RS): K1, ssk,
knit to last 3 stitches, k2tog, k1.
Work even in stockinette stitch for
3 (3, 3, 1) rows.

Size 4 only: Work decrease row.
Work 3 rows stockinette stitch.

All sizes: Repeat decrease row on
next and every following right side
row 14 (16, 16, 20, 21) times more–
57 (56, 57, 54, 55) sts, ending with
a wrong side row.

SHAPE NECK

Next row (RS): K14 (14, 14, 13, 13)
stitches for right front, bind off 29
(28, 29, 28, 29) stitches for front
neck, k14 (14, 14, 13, 13) stitches for
left front.

Work left front stitches as
follows: Purl next wrong side row.
Work decrease as established at
armhole edge every right side row
6 times more and decrease one
stitch at neck edge every 4 (4, 4,
6, 6) rows 3 (3, 3, 2, 2) times–5
stitches.

Next row (RS): K1, sl 1, k2tog, psso,
k1.

Next row: Purl.

Next row (RS): Sl 1, k2tog, psso.

Pull yarn through the remaining
stitch.

Rejoin yarn and work right front
stitches as for left front.

Sleeves (make 2)

With CC1 and smaller needles, cast
on 39 (39, 41, 41, 41) stitches. Work
in k1, p1 rib, ending with k1, for
1¼" (3cm), ending with a wrong
side row. Change to MC and larger
needles.

Next (increase) row (RS): K1, M1, knit to last stitch, M1, k1.

All sizes: Increase every 6th row a total of 7 (10, 7, 12, 13) times and every following 8th row a total of 1 (0, 3, 0, 0) times−55 (59, 61, 65, 67) sts. Work even in stockinette stitch until piece measures 8½ (9½, 10½, 11, 11½)" [22 (24, 27, 28, 29)cm].

SHAPE CAP

Work as for Armhole Shaping on Back. Bind off remaining 13 (13, 13, 11, 11) stitches.

Finishing

Sew Sleeves in place. Sew side and sleeve seams.

NECK TRIM

With CC1 and circular needles, pick up and knit 104 (106, 108, 110, 110) stitches around neck opening. Work in k1, p1 rib for ¾" (2cm). Bind off loosely. Weave in ends. Block.

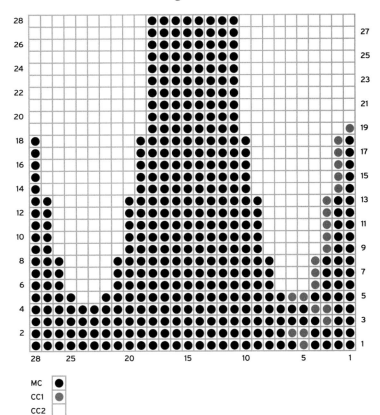

Fang Chart

MC	●
CC1	●
CC2	○

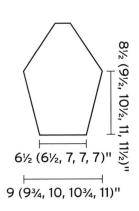

8½ (9½, 10½, 11, 11½)"

6½ (6½, 7, 7, 7)"

9 (9¾, 10, 10¾, 11)"

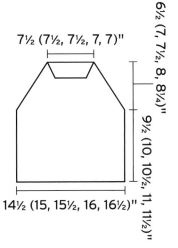

7½ (7½, 7½, 7, 7)"

6½ (7, 7½, 8, 8¼)"

9½ (10, 10½, 11, 11½)"

14½ (15, 15½, 16, 16½)"

4

BLOODY ACCENTS

A pair of fangs and a cape may have been fine for Dracula, but a modern vampire girl knows that the right accessories complete the look. After all, there's really no point in going out on a rampage—or a rescue mission if you swing that way—without a cute purse and alluring jewelry.

You can knit a a fun pillow that trumpets your new diet or a tote that reminds you to keep yourself safe from the supernatural forces out in the world—or you can personalize it to show whose team you're on. Perhaps you'll make a pair of earrings that resemble drops of blood, or a delicate crocheted bracelet that reminds you of the blood you crave, or even a bottle cozy that reveals your blood type.

"Got Blood?" Pillow

If you've just been turned, you probably won't need a reminder of your thirst, but this pillow won't let you forget. If you merely dream of eternal love with the likes of Edward or Damon, this pillow is the perfect accessory for you.

DESIGNED BY → Tanis Gray   SKILL LEVEL → Intermediate

SIZE
One size

FINISHED MEASUREMENTS
12" (30cm) square, excluding edging

MATERIALS
Cascade Venezia Worsted (4) medium (70% merino wool, 30% silk; 3½ oz/100g, 219yds/200m): 2 skeins in 110 Natural (A) and 1 skein in 120 Black (B) → Tahki Yarns/Tahki Stacy Charles Montana (5) bulky (100% unprocessed pure new wool; 3½ oz/100g, 130 yd/120m): 1 skein in 5 Ebony (C) → Size 7 (4.5mm) straight needles → Set of 2 size 15 (10mm) double-pointed needles or short straight needles → Tapestry needle → 12" (30cm) square pillow form

GAUGE
20 stitches and 25 rows = 4" (10cm) in stockinette stitch using smaller needles and A

SPECIAL SKILLS
→ Duplicate stitch (page 135)

STITCH PATTERN
LACE EDGING
Cast on 5 stitches.
Row 1 (RS): K2, yo, k3–6 sts.
Row 2: K6.
Row 3: K2, yo, k4–7 sts.
Row 4: K7.
Row 5: K2, yo, k2tog, [yo] 3 times, k3–10 sts.
Row 6: K3, [k1, p1, k1] in triple yo, k4.
Row 7: K2, yo, k8–11 sts.
Row 8: Bind off 6 stitches, k4–5 sts.
Repeat Rows 1-8 for pattern.

Pillow Front and Back (make 2)
With smaller needles and A, cast on 60 stitches.
Knit 10 rows (work in garter stitch).
Row 1 (RS): Knit.
Row 2: K6, p48, k6.
Repeat Rows 1 and 2 for 11" (28cm).
Knit 10 rows. Bind off.

Finishing
Weave in ends. Block to finished measurements. With B and one pillow piece, work the text from the chart (page 90) in duplicate stitch. With A, sew the pillow front and back together on three sides. Insert the pillow form and sew the last side closed.

Edging
With larger needles and C, work Lace Edging pattern until piece measures approximately 48" (122cm), or as long as needed to wrap around the perimeter of the pillow. Bind off the trim and sew to the pillow edges. Sew the bound-off edge to the cast-on edge. Weave in ends.

Got Blood? Chart

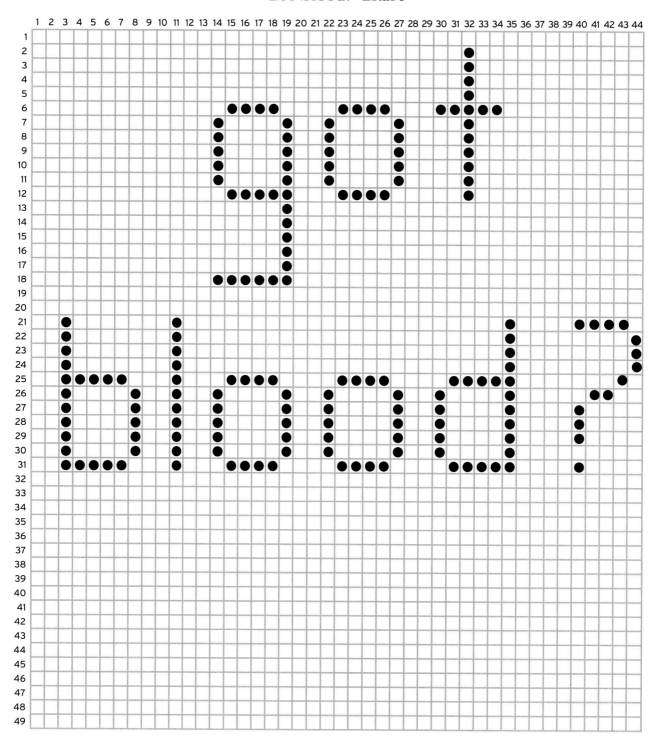

· BLOOD · AND YARN

WHETHER YOU'RE A VAMPIRE OR A HUMAN WHO KEEPS COMPANY WITH THE UNDEAD, YOU MIGHT KEEP THE BLOOD FACTOR IN MIND WHEN CHOOSING FIBERS FOR YOUR KNIT AND CROCHET PROJECTS.

Yarn facts:

While there are no truly stain-resistant yarns, here are some things to know if you should need to wash out blood in a hurry.

 Machine-washable fibers are the best for getting a blood (or other) stain out quickly. Make sure to read the labels on your yarn to see whether it can be washed in the machine.

Most acrylic, polyester, microfiber, and cotton yarns and blends of the fibers are machine washable.

If wool is your favorite fiber, or if your project calls for wool, make sure it's washable. The word "superwash" is a clue.

If the yarn you crave says handwash only, see some of the tips at right on how best to get out stains.

Tips for getting blood out of your clothes:

If you find yourself spending time with blood-suckers—or maybe you've just been turned—you might find you're coming home with a few blood-stains on your clothes. Never fear! Here are a few things to help keep your clothes nice and clean.

For most items, soaking the garment in cold water should do the trick.

If that doesn't work, try putting a little soap straight on the stain and soaking the garment for 15 minutes in warm water that has a tablespoon of ammonia added to it.

Try to soak up the stain by drenching it with water and blotting with a towel, using moderate pressure.

If these suggestions don't work, you can always soak the whole garment in blood to make it a nice even shade of red!

Vampire Totes

Share your love for vampires or werewolves with these knitted totes inspired by TWILIGHT. Follow the charts to show what team you're on, or use the alphabet to create your own design.

DESIGNED BY → Marilee Norris   SKILL LEVEL → Intermediate

ALPHABET & "BE SAFE" CHARTS BY → Marilee Norris
"TEAM EDWARD" & "TEAM JACOB" CHARTS BY → Ashley Fay

SIZE
One size

FINISHED MEASUREMENTS
11" x 11½" (28cm x 29cm)

MATERIALS
FOR ALL VERSIONS
Size 7 (4.5mm) straight needles → Tapestry needle → 45" (114cm) ¼" (0.5cm) wide satin ribbon → 12" x 23" (30cm x 58cm) piece of satin lining fabric → Sewing needle and matching thread (for lining)

BE SAFE VERSION
Lion Brand Wool-Ease Worsted  medium (80% acrylic, 20% wool; 3 oz/85g, 197 yd/180m): 2 skeins in Black [MC] → Lion Brand Wool-Ease Worsted (4) medium (80% acrylic, 20% wool; 3 oz/85g, 197 yd/180m): 1 skein in Ranch Red [CC] → Red metallic sewing thread (for couching)

TEAM EDWARD VERSION
Lion Brand Wool-Ease Worsted (4) medium (80% acrylic, 20% wool; 3 oz/85g, 197 yd/180m): 2 skeins in Black [MC] → Lion Brand Wool-Ease Worsted Multi (4) medium (78% acrylic, 19% wool, 3% polyester; 2½ oz/70g, 162 yd/146m): 1 skein in White/Multi [CC] → White sewing thread (for couching)

TEAM JACOB VERSION
Lion Brand Wool-Ease Worsted (4) medium (80% acrylic, 20% wool; 3 oz/85g, 197 yd/180m): 2 skeins in Black [MC] → Lion Brand Wool-Ease Worsted (4) medium (80% acrylic, 20% wool; 3 oz/85g, 197 yd/180m): 1 skein in Chestnut Heather [CC] → Brown sewing thread (for couching)

GAUGE
20 stitches and 26 rows = 4" (10cm) in stockinette stitch

SPECIAL SKILLS
→ **Stranded knitting (page 134) or duplicate stitch (page 135)**

NOTE
Using CC and following the chart motifs, work in stranded knitting or duplicate stitch as desired. For the embroidery (elements not confined to the chart grid), use CC and couching thread as described on page 94.

· TID-BITE ·
The most famous early vampire movies are the 1922 film NOSFERATU, starring Max Shreck, and Bela Lugosi's famous rendition of DRACULA in 1931. More recent popular movies include Joel Shumacher's THE LOST BOYS in 1987 and the 1992 Francis Ford Copolla movie BRAM STOKER'S DRACULA starring Gary Oldman.

Bag

With MC, cast on 60 stitches. Work in stockinette stitch for 2" (5cm), ending with a wrong side row.

Next (picot) row (RS): K1, *k2tog, yo; repeat from * to last stitch, k1. Work in stockinette stitch until piece measures 3" (8cm) from cast-on edge, ending with a wrong side row.

Next (eyelet) row (RS): *K3, k2tog, yo; repeat from * to last 5 stitches, k5.

Note: If you want the chart design to be on both sides of the bag, begin the first chart when piece measures 4" (10cm). Center chart over the piece (10 stitches in from each edge), being careful to begin the first chart from Row 52, to ensure design isn't upside down! If you are not working the chart on both sides, work even in stockinette stitch. For both, work until piece measures 15" (38cm), ending with a wrong side row.

BEGIN CHART

Centering chart over the piece, work beginning with Row 1. Once chart is complete, work even in stockinette stitch until the piece measures 24" (61cm), ending with a wrong side row.

Next (eyelet) row (RS): *K3, k2tog, yo; repeat from * to last 5 stitches, k5.

Work even in stockinette stitch for 1" (2.5cm) more, ending with a wrong side row.

Next (picot) row (RS): K1, *k2tog, yo; repeat from * to last stitch, k1. Work even in stockinette stitch for 2" (5cm) more. Bind off. Piece measures 27" (69cm).

Strap

With MC, cast on 12 stitches.

Row 1 (RS): *K1, YF, sl 1, YB; repeat from * across.

Row 2: *P1, YB, sl 1, YF; repeat from * across.

Repeat Rows 1 and 2 until piece measures 24" (61cm). Bind off.

Finishing

Weave in ends.

EMBROIDERY

To begin the couching, bring the yarn up through the back of the knitting, and lay it across the top of your work in the shape of your intended design, using the designs on the chart as a general guide. Then, with matching sewing thread, stitch the yarn in place at regular intervals. When you are finished with your design, take the yarn back through to the wrong side of your work and weave in the ends.

SEAMING

Sew side seams with MC and tapestry needle. Weave in ends. Thread ribbon through the eyelet row and tie in a bow.

LINING

Fold lining fabric in half, with right sides together. Using sewing needle and thread, sew side seams ½" (1cm) in from edges. Fold top of lining down ½" (1cm) and sew in place. Place in bag. Fold knitted hem of bag along picot rows over top edges of the lining and sew in place.

Sew strap to side seams of the bag.

· EMBROIDERY STITCHES ·

- Couching: A technique in which yarn or thread is laid across the surface of the knitted fabric and held in place with small stitches of a lighter weight yarn or sewing thread.

- Cross stitch: A technique that uses two stitches to form a cross or X over a knit stitch.

- Duplicate stitch (page 135): A technique in which you make a stitch in a contrasting color that duplicates the knitted stitch. The result looks like the stitches were knitted into the fabric.

Lower Case Alphabet

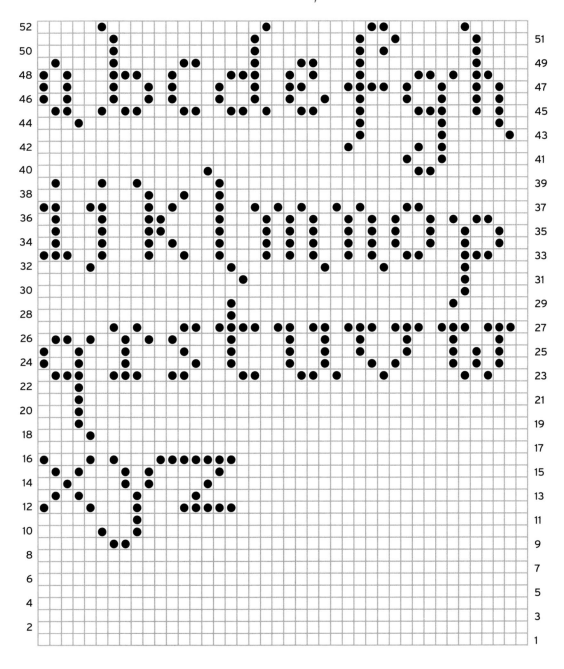

Upper Case Alphabet

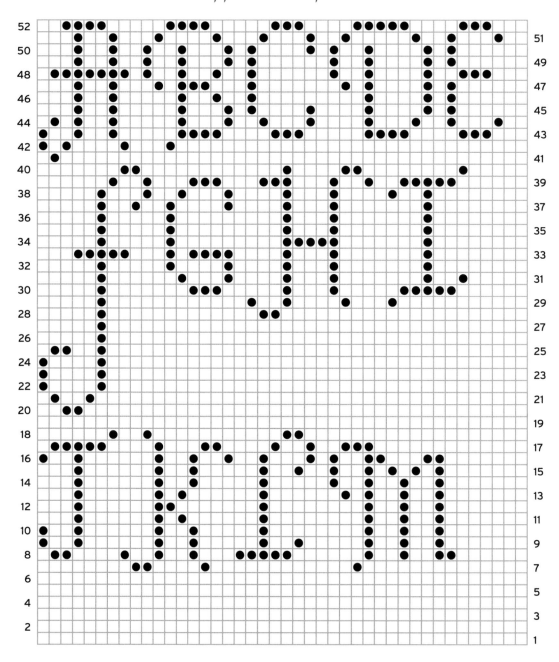

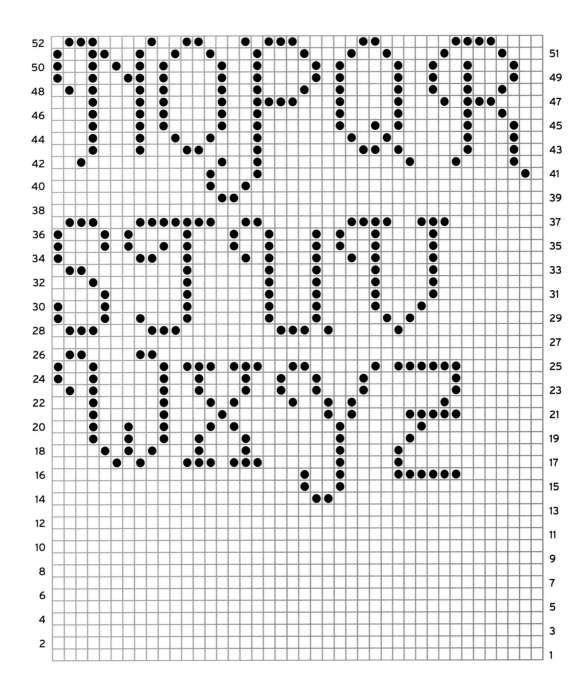

Be Safe Chart

Team Edward Chart

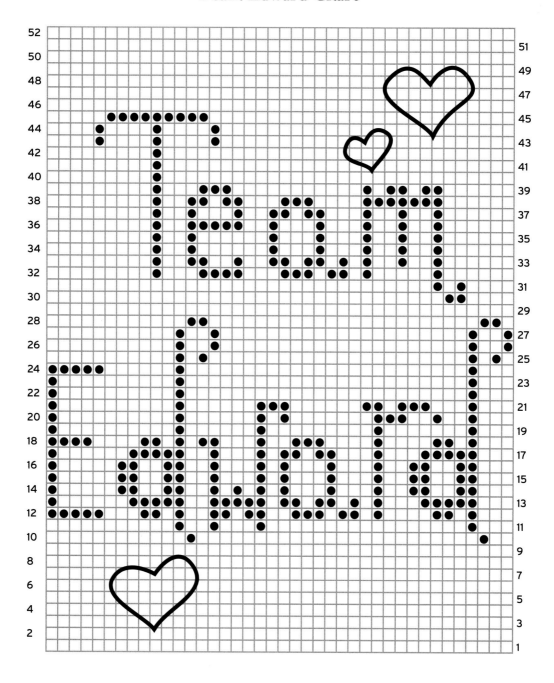

Team Jacob Chart

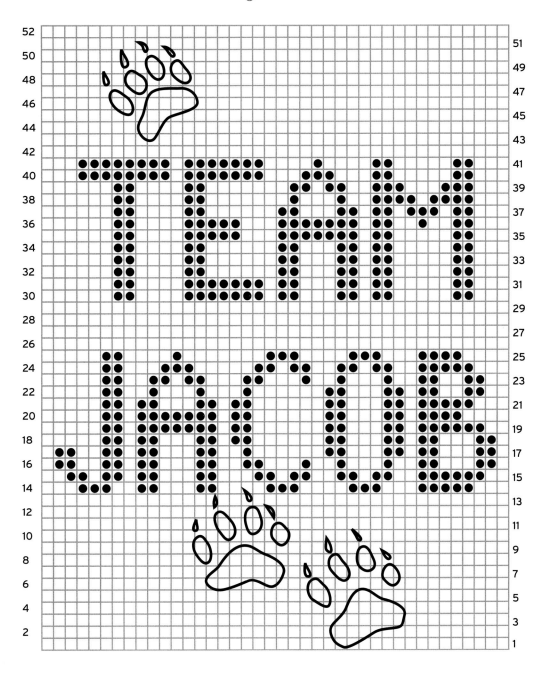

Glamour Earrings and Sangria Bracelet

The name of the earrings plays on a double meaning of the word glamour: beauty and style OR the ability of a vampire to hypnotize a human into submission with a simple but effective stare. The gradient effect of the bracelet yarn is reminiscent of sangria, the root word of which translates as "blood."

DESIGNED BY → Kimberly Dijkstra   SKILL LEVEL → Intermediate

SIZE
One size

FINISHED MEASUREMENTS
Earrings: ⅝" x 1" (1.5cm x 2.5cm), excluding earwires
Bracelet: 1¼" x 6¼" (3cm x 16cm), excluding chain and clasp

MATERIALS
For the earrings: DMC six-strand Embroidery Floss (100% long-staple double-mercerized cotton; 8.7 yd/8m): 1 skein in color 115 → Size 5 (1.9mm) steel crochet hook → Six 5mm Gütermann teardrop beads in 4395 Raspberry → Tapestry needle → 2 ear wires → 2 jump rings → Needle-nose pliers

For the bracelet: DMC six-strand Embroidery Floss (100% long-staple double-mercerized cotton; 8.7 yd/8m): 2 skeins in color 115 → Size 5 (1.9mm) steel crochet hook → Tapestry needle → 2 eyepins → Round-nosed pliers → 2 jump rings → 1 spring-ring clasp

GAUGE
1 bracelet motif = 1¼" (3cm) square
Gauge is not essential for the earrings.

SPECIAL INSTRUCTIONS
→ **Ch 1 w/bead:** Slide bead to hook, chain 1, trapping the bead in place.

NOTE
The earrings are made by working 6 double crochet stitches up until the last loop, then drawing the thread through all the loops on the hook.

· TID-BITE ·

The term "vamp" became popular after the actress Theda Bara starred in several vampire movies in the early 1900s. Her characters often drained their suitors of both money and affection.

Earring (make 2)

String 3 beads onto floss.

Row 1: [Ch 1, ch 1 w/ bead] 3 times, ch 3, turn.

Row 2: Yo, insert hook into the back loop of the 4th stitch from the hook, yo, draw through loop, yo, draw through 2 loops on hook, yo, draw through 1 loop on hook, [yo, insert hook into the back loop of the next stitch, yo, draw through the loop, yo, draw through 2 loops on hook, yo, draw through 1 loop on hook] 5 times, yo, draw through all loops on hook, ch 1. Fasten off.

Finishing

Weave in ends.

Open jump ring, slip it under ch-1 at the top of the earring, add the ear wire, close jump ring.

· TID-BITE ·

The English word "vampire" is thought to have come from the Serbian VAMPIR or UPIR. In some languages, werewolves are synonymous with vampires, and the more modern Slavic term for vampire, VUKODLAK, is also their word for werewolf. Similarly, the Greek VRYKOLAKAS, very similar to the Lithuanian VILKOLAKIS, means "vampire" and "werewolf."

· CROCHET STITCHES ·

- **CH 1:** With a slip knot on the hook, yo and draw through the loop already on the hook.

- **SC:** Insert the hook into the stitch, pull up a loop of yarn, yo, and pull the yarn through both loops on the hook.

- **DC:** Yo, insert the hook into the stitch, pulling up a loop (three loops on the hook). Yo, draw through the first two loops on the hook, yo, and draw through the last two loops on the hook.

- **SL ST:** Insert the hook into the stitch, yo, and pull a loop through both the stitch and the loop on the hook.

- **YO:** Wrap the yarn around the hook before inserting the hook into a stitch.

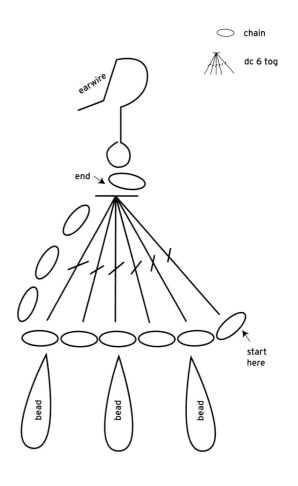

Bracelet

MOTIF 1

Ch 7, join in ring with sl st.

Round 1: 12 sc in ring, join with sl st.

Round 2: [Ch 6, skip 2 sc, sl st in next sc] 4 times.

Round 3: [(4 sc in ch-6 space, ch 3) twice, 4 sc] 4 times, join with sl st. Fasten off, weave in ends.

MOTIF 2

Work as for Motif 1 through Round 2.

Round 3: 4 sc in ch-6 space, ch 3, 4 sc, ch 1, sl st in 1st picot of Motif 1, ch 1, 4 sc, 4 sc in next ch-6 space, ch 1, sl st in 8th picot of Motif 1, ch 1, 4 sc, ch 3, 4 sc, [(4 sc in next ch-6 space, ch 3) twice, 4 sc], join with sl st. Fasten off, weave in ends.

MOTIF 3

Work as for Motif 1 through Round 2.

Round 3: 4 sc in ch-6 space, ch 3, 4 sc, ch 1, sl st in 5th picot of Motif 1, ch 1, 4 sc, 4 sc in next ch-6 space, ch 1, sl st in 4th picot of Motif 1, ch 1, 4 sc, ch 3, 4 sc, [(4 sc in next ch-6 space, ch 3) twice, 4 sc], join with sl st. Fasten off, weave in ends.

MOTIF 4

Work as for Motif 1 through Round 2.

Round 3: 4 sc in ch-6 space, ch 3, 4 sc, ch 1, sl st in 7th picot of Motif 2, ch 1, 4 sc, 4 sc in next ch-6 space, ch 1, sl st in 6th picot of Motif 2, ch 1, 4 sc, ch 3, 4 sc, [(4 sc in next ch-6 space, ch 3) twice, 4 sc], join with sl st. Fasten off, weave in ends.

MOTIF 5

Work as for Motif 1 through Round 2.

Round 3: 4 sc in ch-6 space, ch 3, 4 sc, ch 1, sl st in 6th picot of Motif 3, ch 1, 4 sc, 4 sc in next ch-6 space, ch 1, sl st in 7th picot of Motif 3, ch 1, 4 sc, ch 3, 4 sc, [(4 sc in next ch-6 space, ch 3) twice, 4 sc], join with sl st. Fasten off, weave in ends.

Finishing

Insert eyepin into 7th and 8th picot of Motif 4. Use round-nosed pliers to create a loop on the other side of eyepin. Cut a length of chain with an odd number of links. Attach each end of chain to each loop of eyepin. Attach jump ring to middle link and attach the clasp to jump ring. Repeat for Motif 5.

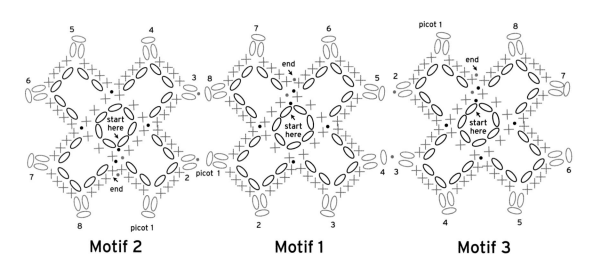

Motif 2　　　　**Motif 1**　　　　**Motif 3**

Chain Rnd
Rnd 1
Rnd 2
Rnd 3

- chain
- • slip stitch
- ✕ single crochet

A MODERN GIRL'S GUIDE TO
VAMPIRES

Things you should have on hand to ward off a vampire:

→ **Mirrors:** Since according to legend they can't be seen in a mirror, vampires tend to stay away from them. Mirrors may also help to deflect their powers of hypnotism.

→ **Garlic:** Garlic has been used as a deterrent for vampires for centuries most likely started in Romania. (Of, course, if you want vampires around, modern vamps like the ones who live in Bon Temps, Louisiana, don't seem to mind it too much!)

→ **Seeds:** In old vampire stories, bloodsuckers are described as a bit compulsive. If seeds are spilled on the ground, they'll spend hours counting each and every one of them.

→ **Matches:** One proven way to kill vampires is by fire, so matches tend to keep them away.

→ **Religious items:** Holy water, crosses, crucifixes ...

Ways to identify a vampire:

→ He has pale skin.

→ He's cold to the touch.

→ He only comes out at night—or if he does hang out in the daytime, look for a special ring, or a sparkle to his skin.

→ He doesn't age. If you've known a guy for several years and he always looks exactly the same, he may very well be a vamp.

→ Of course, if he has extremely sharp canines or goes a little insane if you get a paper cut, that might be a real tip off.

Blood Bottle Cozies

Keep your drink at a perfect 98.6 degrees when you're at Merlotte's with these Fair Isle bottle cozies, and of course, personalize them with your blood type.

DESIGNED BY → Tanis Gray SKILL LEVEL → Intermediate

SIZE
One size, will fit most 12 oz soda or beverage bottles

FINISHED MEASUREMENTS
Approximately 3½" high x 8" circumference (9cm x 20cm), after blocking

MATERIALS
Plymouth Dreambaby DK (3) light (50% acrylic microfiber, 50% nylon; 1¾ oz/50g, 183 yd/167m): 1 skein each in 108 Red (A), 118 Ecru (B), 113 Black (C) → Size 6 (4mm) straight needles → Spare Size 6 (4mm) needle → Size G-6 (4mm) crochet hook → Waste yarn → Tapestry needle

GAUGE
22 stitches and 22 rows = 4" (10cm) in Fair Isle pattern, after blocking

SPECIAL SKILLS
→ **Stranded knitting (page 134)**
→ **Duplicate stitch (page 135)**
→ **3-Needle bind-off (page 135)**

NOTE
The bottle cozies are knit from side to side and the letters are added in duplicate stitch after knitting is completed.

Bottle Cozy
Select the desired chart (pages 110, 112, 113).
With waste yarn and a crochet hook, work a chain slightly longer than 21 stitches. Fasten off.
With the first color needed, pick up and knit 21 stitches from the chain.
Following the chart, work in stockinette stitch, loosely stranding the color not in use on the wrong side. When the chart is complete, leave the stitches on the needle. Unzip the crochet chain and place the live stitches on a second needle. Add letters using duplicate stitch, following the chart.

Finishing
Weave in ends. Block. Fold piece in half with wrong side facing. Join the bound-off edge to the cast-on edge using a 3-needle bind-off.

· TID-BITE ·

The first "reluctant" vampire was Barnabas Collins from DARK SHADOWS in 1966. Following him and also wishing to change their ways are BUFFY THE VAMPIRE SLAYER's Angel, THE VAMPIRE DIARIES' Stefan Salvatore, TWILIGHT's Edward Cullen and his "family," and some of Charlaine Harris's Louisiana vampires who've taken to drinking synthetic blood.

Blood Type Charts

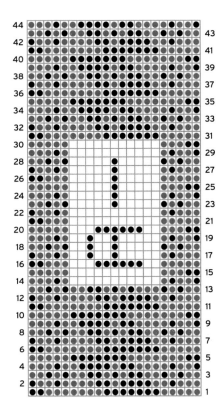

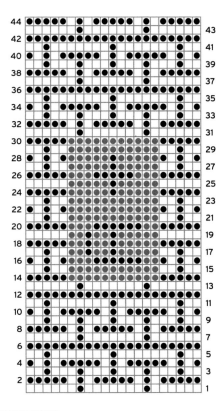

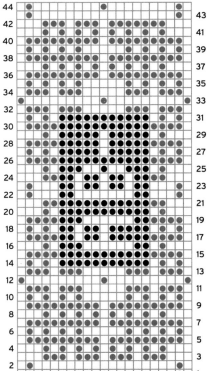

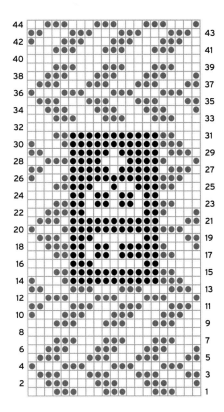

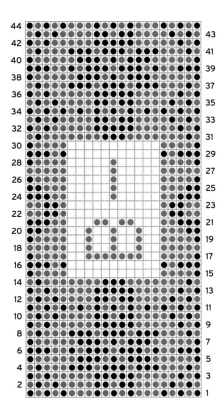

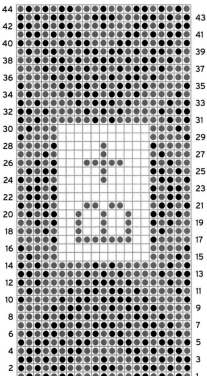

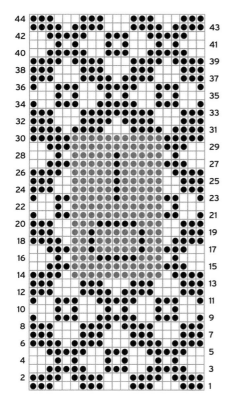

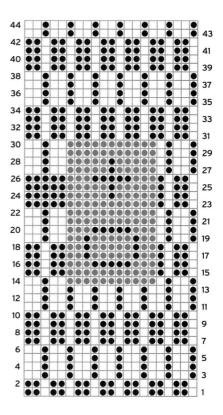

5

WHO'S AFRAID OF THE BIG, BAD WOLF?

Where there are vampires it seems there have always been werewolves and other shape-shifters. Whether they're furry warriors for good, like Jacob or Oz, or shifters both good and bad in Bon Temps and Shreveport, Louisiana, they provide a contrast and comple-ment to the vampires in our midst. Some of them shift their shapes under the power of a full moon; others assume animal form at will. Sometimes we might even be tempted to love them as much if not more than the mysterious—and less hairy—vamps.

Wherever you pledge your heart, werewolves are almost as intriguing as vampires, and they've given us a lot of inspiration as well. In this chapter, you'll find projects for humans and wolves alike. With a pair of paw warmers, a shapeshifting shrug, a furry pillow to cuddle up with, and a warm wolfy hat for you and the little pups in your life,

Paw Warmers

Whether you're a human or a shapeshifter, keep your paws warm with these cute fingerless gloves.

DESIGNED BY → Teri Christensen   SKILL LEVEL → Intermediate

SIZE
Woman's Small/Medium (Woman's Large/Men's Small)

FINISHED MEASUREMENTS
7½ (9)" [19 (22)cm] circumference

MATERIALS
KnitPicks Merino Style (3) light (100% wool; 1¾ oz/50g, 123 yd/112m): 1 skein each in Nutmeg [MC] and Cinnamon [CC] → Set of 5 size 5 (3.75mm) double-pointed needles → Waste yarn → Stitch markers → Tapestry needle → Size D (3.25mm) crochet hook

GAUGE
24 stitches and 32 rows = 4" (10cm) in stockinette stitch

SPECIAL SKILLS
→ Duplicate stitch (page 135)

SPECIAL INSTRUCTIONS
→ M1R: From the back, lift loop between stitches with the left needle, knit into front of loop.

→ M1L: From the front, lift loop between stitches with the left needle, knit into back of loop.

Cuff
With MC, cast on 44 (52) stitches, dividing stitches as evenly as possible over 3 needles.

Place marker and join in a round. Work in k1, p1 rib for 2 (2½)" [5 (6)cm].

Next round: *K1, p1; repeat from * to last 2 stitches, k1, kfb–45 (53) stitches.

Thumb Gusset
Arrange stitches as follows on next round:
Needle 1: K16 (18).
Needle 2: K6 (8), pm, M1L, k1, M1R, pm, k6 (8).
Needle 3: K16 (18)–47 (55) stitches.
Knit 1 round in stockinette stitch.
*Next (increase) round: Knit to marker, slip marker, M1L, knit to next marker, M1R, slip marker, knit to end.
Work 2 rounds even. Repeat from * a total of 6 (7) times, until there are 15 (17) gusset stitches between the markers.

Hand
Arrange the stitches as follows on next round:
Needle 1: K11 (13).
Needle 2: K11 (13).
Needle 3: Remove the markers and slip 15 (17) gusset stitches onto waste yarn. Cast on 1 stitch over the gap, k10 (12).
Needle 4: K12 (14)–45 (53) stitches.
Work even in stockinette stitch until stockinette portion measures 3½ (3¾)" [9 (9.5)cm].

LITTLE FINGER
K6 (7), place 34 (40) stitches on waste yarn and cast on 1 stitch over the gap. On a new needle, knit to the end of the round: 12 (14) stitches for finger. Rearrange these 12 (14) stitches evenly on 3 double-pointed needles. *K1, p1; repeat

from * around for 4 rounds, then bind off loosely.

UPPER HAND
Remove stitches from waste yarn and arrange as follows on 4 double-pointed needles:
Needle 1: 9 (10) stitches.
Needle 2: 8 (10) stitches.
Needle 3: 8 (10) stitches.
Needle 4: 9 (10) stitches—34 (40) stitches.
Rejoin yarn at the gap by the little finger. With a crochet hook, pick up 2 stitches at base of little finger and add to the stitches on Needle 4—36 (42) stitches.
Knit 3 rounds.

RING FINGER
K6 (7), place 24 (28) stitches on waste yarn and cast on 1 stitch over the gap. On a new needle, knit to end of the round—13 (15) stitches for finger. Rearrange the stitches evenly on 3 double-pointed needles. *K1, p1; repeat from * around to last stitch. Knit this last stitch together with the first stitch—12 (14) stitches remain. *K1, p1; repeat from * around for 3 more rounds, then bind off loosely.

MIDDLE FINGER
Remove the first 6 (7) and last 6 (7) stitches from the waste yarn onto 2 double-pointed needles (leaving remaining stitches on waste yarn). Rejoin the yarn at

the gap by the ring finger. With a crochet hook, pick up 2 stitches at the base of the ring finger and put these stitches on a new needle (new Needle 1). K6 (7) onto the new Needle 1, cast on 1 stitch over the gap and knit to the end of the round [15 (17) stitches for finger]. Rearrange the stitches evenly on 3 double-pointed needles. *K1, p1; repeat from * around to last stitch. Knit this last stitch together with the first stitch—14 (16) stitches remain. *K1, p1; repeat from * around for 3 more rounds, then bind off loosely.

INDEX FINGER
Remove remaining 12 (14) stitches from the waste yarn onto 2 double-pointed needles—6 (7) stitches on each needle. Rejoin the yarn at the gap by the middle finger. With a crochet hook, pick up 2 stitches at base of the middle finger and put these stitches on a new needle (new Needle 1). Knit to end of round—14 (16) stitches.
Rearrange the stitches evenly on 3 double-pointed needles. *K1, p1; repeat from * around for 4 rounds, then bind off loosely.

THUMB
Remove remaining 15 (17) stitches from

the waste yarn and arrange onto 2 double-pointed needles. Rejoin the yarn at the gap by the index finger and with crochet hook, pick up 1 stitch at the base of the index finger and put this stitch on a new needle (new Needle 1). Knit to the end of round—16 (18) stitches. Rearrange the stitches evenly on 3 double-pointed needles. *K1, p1; repeat from * around for 4 rounds. Bind off loosely.

Finishing
Weave in ends, making sure to close up any gaps or holes between the fingers.

PAW PRINT PATTERN
Using CC and either cross stitch or duplicate stitch embroider the paw print pattern on the palm side of one or both mitts. Begin the colored portion of the chart approximately 3 rows above the ribbed cuff.

Paw Print Chart

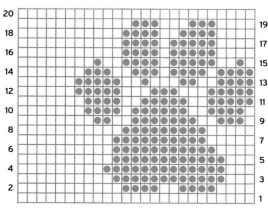

Shapeshifter Shrug

Inspired by the idea of a shapeshifter that can change itself to be appropriate for any situation, this piece can be worn in multiple ways: Button each sleeve to wear it as a shrug, give it a half twist and button the ends together to wear it as a möbius shawl, or wear it unbuttoned as a scarf.

DESIGNED BY → Sara Delaney   SKILL LEVEL → Intermediate

SIZE
One size fits most

FINISHED MEASUREMENTS
22" x 48" (56cm x 122cm)

MATERIALS
Berroco Peruvia (4) medium (100% Peruvian highland wool; 3½ oz/100g, 174 yd/160m): 4 skeins in 7114 Chipotle → Size 9 (5.5mm) straight or circular needles → Stitch holders or waste yarn → Tapestry needle → Twenty ⅞" (2.2cm) buttons

GAUGE
20 stitches and 24 rows = 4" (10cm) in stockinette stitch, after blocking

· TID-BITE ·

SUCCUBI are female vampires who seduce human men, drawing energy for themselves and draining the men, sometimes tricking innocents into impregnating them.

STITCH PATTERN
GRAPEVINE PATTERN

In this pattern, stitches are decreased on Rows 2 and 8 and increased on Rows 6 and 12.

Row 1 and all WS rows: Purl.

Row 2: K2, *k2tog, k1, yo, k1, ssk, k2; repeat from *, end k4.

Row 4: K1, k2tog, k1, yo, *k1, yo, k1, ssk, k2tog, k1, yo; repeat from *, end k2.

Row 6: K3, yo, *k3, yo, k1, ssk, k1, yo; repeat from *, end k3.

Row 8: K5, *k2tog, k1, yo, k1, ssk, k2; repeat from *, end k2.

Row 10: K4, *k2tog, k1, [yo, k1] twice, ssk; repeat from *, end k3.

Row 12: K3, k2tog, *k1, yo, k3, yo, k1, k2tog; repeat from *, end k2.

Repeat Rows 1–12 for pattern.

NOTE
The garment is worked in two pieces and joined in the center back with Kitchener stitch; this allows you to adjust the length for a more custom fit. Knit the first and last five stitches of every row to create a garter stitch border.

First Half
Cast on 96 stitches.

Knit 5 rows.

Row 6 (RS): K1, bind off next 3 stitches for the buttonhole, k1, pm, k86, pm, k5.

Row 7: K5, work Row 1 of the Grapevine Pattern over the next 86 stitches, cast on 3 stitches over the gap to close the buttonhole, k1.

Rows 8-54: Work as established, working a buttonhole as before every 12 rows for a total of 10 buttonholes. (Continue buttonholes on next section until all are worked.)

Row 55-end: Maintaining the garter stitch border, work center 86 stitches in stockinette stitch until piece measures approximately 24" (61cm) or desired length. Place the stitches on a holder or waste yarn and set aside.

Second Half

Cast on 96 stitches.
Knit 5 rows.
Row 6 (RS): K1, pm, k86, pm, k1, bind off 3 stitches for the buttonhole, k1.
Row 7: K1, cast on 3 stitches over the gap to close the buttonhole, k1, work Row 1 of the Grapevine Pattern over the next 86 stitches, k5.
Continue as for First Half, working the buttonholes as established.

Finishing

Graft the pieces together using the Kitchener stitch. Weave in the ends. Sew the buttons opposite the buttonholes.

Werewolf Hat

If you're feeling the Full Moon calling to you, put on this hat to expose your inner wolf. Or, make one for the little pups in your life!

DESIGNED BY → Abigail Horsfall   SKILL LEVEL → Intermediate

SIZE
Toddler (Child, Small Adult, Large Adult)

FINISHED MEASUREMENTS
Fits head circumference 16 (18, 20, 22)" [41(46, 51, 56)cm]

MATERIALS
Knitpicks Suri Dream 6 super bulky (74% Suri Alpaca, 22% Peruvian Highland Wool, 4% Nylon; 1¾ oz/50g, 143 yd/130m): 1 skein in Fedora (child) or Black Forest (adult size) → Set of 5 size 10.5 (6.5mm) double-pointed needles → Stitch markers → Tapestry needle

GAUGE
13 stitches and 20 rows = 4" (10cm) in stockinette stitch

• TID-BITE •

An Eastern European belief was that those who are shapeshifters become vampires when they die.

Hat
Cast on 54 (60, 66, 72) stitches. Place marker and join in the round.
Round 1: Purl.
Round 2: Knit.
Round 3: Purl.
Round 4: Knit.
Round 5: Purl.
Round 6: Knit.
Continue to knit, working in the round, until hat measures 3½ (4, 4½, 5)" [9 (10, 11.5, 12.5)cm] from cast-on edge.
Work crown decreases:
Begin with Round 7 (5, 3, 1).
Round 1: *K10, k2tog* 6 times.
Rounds 2, 4, 6, 8, 10: Knit.
Round 3: *K1, ssk, k8* 6 times.
Round 5: *K8, k2tog* 6 times.
Round 7: *K1, ssk, k6* 6 times.
Round 9: *K6, k2tog* 6 times.
Round 11: *K1, ssk, k4* 6 times.
Round 12: *K4, k2tog* 6 times.
Round 13: *K1, ssk, k2* 6 times.
Round 14: *K2, k2tog* 6 times.
Round 15: *K1, ssk* 6 times.
Break yarn and thread through remaining stitches. Pull tight.

Wolf Ears (make 2)

Note: Using 2 strands of yarn will make the ears thicker, so they stand up better, but is not necessary.

Cast on one stitch.

Row 1: Kfb (2 stitches)

All even rows: Purl.

Row 3: Kfb, kfb–4 stitches.

Row 5: Kfb, k2, kfb–6 stitches.

Row 7: Kfb, k4, kfb–8 stitches.

Row 9: Kfb, k6, kfb–10 stitches.

*For Adult and Large Adult add one more increase row: kfb, k8, kfb–12 stitches.

Row 11: Knit.

Row 13: Knit.

Bind off. Sew ears to top of hat where desired.

· TID-BITE ·

There aren't many tales of vampire children, and for a good reason. Children aren't fully developed and don't have the self-control of adults, so the idea of an immortal monster trapped in the body of a child seems to violate everything we believe about children. Their innocence, quite literally, would be gone. The most well known child vampire is Claudia, from Anne Rice's INTERVIEW WITH A VAMPIRE, who is eventually killed because she is seen as an abomination.

Earflaps (make 2)

With right side facing, pick up 14 (16, 18, 20) stitches from the cast-on edge, centered over the beginning of the round (use your yarn tail to determine this point if necessary; it should also be centered under a wolf ear).

Row 1: Knit.

Row 2: K1, k2tog, knit to last 3 stitches, ssk, k1.

Repeat Rows 1 and 2 until 4 stitches remain.

Bind off.

Finishing

TASSELS

Cut 9 strands of yarn about 1 yard (1m) long each (or approximately 2½ times as long as desired) for each ear. Using a tapestry needle, pull the lengths through the bottom center of each earflap, ensuring the yarn is the same length on each side. Divide strands into three sets of six strands on one side and braid. Tie a firm knot, and trim the ends. Repeat for the other side. Weave in ends.

Imprint Pillow

Snuggle with your own cuddly wolf pillow. Soft on one side and furry on the other, it's two-sided—or two-natured—just like a werewolf.

DESIGNED BY → Genevieve Miller   SKILL LEVEL → Easy

SIZE

One size

FINISHED MEASUREMENTS

14" (36cm) square

MATERIALS

Lion Brand Jiffy Yarn (5) bulky (100% brushed acrylic; 3 oz/85g, 135 yd/123m): 2 skeins in 155 Silver Heather [MC] and 1 skein in 152 Charcoal Mist [CC] → Lion Brand Fun Fur Prints (5) bulky (100% polyester; 1½ oz/40g, 57 yd/52m): 2 skeins in 204 Lava → Size 9 (5.5mm) straight needles → Tapestry needle → 14" (36cm) square pillow form

GAUGE

16 stitches = 4" (10cm) in stockinette stitch, using MC

SPECIAL SKILLS

→ Duplicate stitch (page 135)

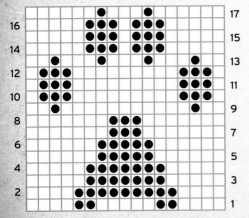

Pillow Front

With MC, cast on 56 stitches. Work in stockinette stitch for 14" (36cm). Bind off. With CC, embroider paw prints in duplicate stitch, following the chart (below, left) and placing the paws as desired on the pillow front.

Pillow Back

With Fun Fur, cast on 56 stitches loosely. Work in stockinette stitch for 13" (33cm). Bind off loosely. The piece will stretch to fit the pillow form.

Finishing

Weave in the ends. Place the panels together, wrong side out. Using Fun Fur, sew the panels together on 3 sides. Turn right side out. Insert the pillow form and sew closed.

Abbreviations

BO → Bind off

C4B → Place 2 stitches on cable needle and hold to back, k2, k2 from cable needle

C4F → Place 2 stitches on cable needle and hold to front, k2, k2 from cable needle

C6B → Slip 3 stitches onto cable needle and hold to back, k3, k3 from cable needle

C6F → Slip 3 stitches onto cable needle and hold to front, k3, k3 from cable needle

CC → Contrasting color

CO → Cast on

K → Knit

K2tog → Knit two stitches together to decrease

Kfb → Knit into the front and the back of the stitch to increase

M1 → Make one stitch

MC → Main color

P → Purl

P2tog → Purl 2 stitches together to decrease

PM → Place marker

Psso → Pass slipped stitch over the stitch you just knit

Ptbl → Purl through the back loop

RS → Right side

S1 → Slip one stitch

SM → Slip marker

SSK → Slip, slip, knit to decrease

T3B → Place 1 stitch on cable needle and hold to back, k2, p1 from cable needle

T3F → Place 2 stitches on cable needle and hold to front, p1, k2 from cable needle

WS → Wrong side

Wyib → With yarn in back

Wyif → With yarn in front

YB → Yarn to the back

YF → Yarn forward

YO → Yarn over

Skill Levels

Easy ⇢ Uses basic stitches, repetitive stitch patterns, and simple color changes. Involves simple shaping and finishing.

Intermediate ⇢ Uses a variety of stitches, such as basic cables and lace, simple intarsia, double-pointed needles, and knitting-in-the-round, with midlevel shaping and finishing.

Experienced ⇢ Involves intricate stitch patterns, techniques, and dimension, such as nonrepeating patterns, multicolored techniques, fine threads, detailed shaping, and refined finishing.

Standard Yarn Weight System

Yarn Weight Category & Symbol	0 LACE	1 SUPER FINE	2 FINE	3 LIGHT	4 MEDIUM	5 BULKY	6 SUPER BULKY
Types of Yarn	Fingering, 10-count crochet thread	Sock, fingering, baby	Sport, baby	DK, light worsted	Worsted, afghan, aran	Chunky, craft, rug	Bulky, roving
Knit Gauge Range (in Stockinette Stitch to 4 inches)	33-40 sts	27-32 sts	23-26 sts	21-24 sts	16-20 sts	12-15 sts	6-11 sts
Recommended needle sizes (U.S./metric sizes)	00-1/1.5-2.25mm	1-3/2.25-3.25mm	3-5/3.25-3.75mm	5-7/3.75-4.5mm	7-9/4.5-5.5mm	9-11/5.5-8mm	11 and larger/8mm and larger

Adapted from the Standard Yarn Weight System of the Craft Yarn Council of America (www.yarnstandards.com)

Metric Conversion Chart

Inches to Centimeters

inches	cm		inches	cm
1/16	0.16		25	63.50
1/8	0.32		26	66.04
3/16	0.48		27	60.58
1/4	0.64		28	71.12
5/16	0.79		29	73.66
3/8	0.95		30	76.20
7/16	1.11		31	78.74
1/2	1.27		32	81.28
9/16	1.43		33	83.82
5/8	1.59		34	86.36
11/16	1.75		35	88.9
3/4	1.91		36	91.44
13/16	2.06		37	93.98
7/8	2.22		38	96.52
15/16	2.38		39	99.06
1	2.54		40	101.60
2	5.08		41	104.14
3	7.65		42	106.68
4	10.16		43	109.22
5	12.70		44	111.76
6	15.24		45	114.30
7	17.78		46	116.84
8	20.32		47	119.38
9	22.66		48	121.92
10	25.40		49	124.46
11	27.94		50	127.00
12	30.48		51	129.54
13	33.02		52	132.08
14	35.56		53	134.62
15	38.10		54	137.16
16	40.64		55	139.70
17	43.18		56	142.24
18	45.72		57	144.78
19	48.26		58	147.32
20	50.80		59	149.86
21	53.34		60	152.40
22	55.88			
23	58.42			
24	60.96			

Centimeters to Inches

cm	inches	cm	inches	cm	inches	cm	inches
1	3/8	40	15 3/4	79	31 1/8	118	46 1/2
2	3/4	41	16 1/8	80	31 1/2	119	46 7/8
3	1 1/8	42	16 1/2	81	31 7/8	120	47 1/4
4	1 5/8	43	16 7/8	82	32+	121	47 5/8
5	2	44	17 1/4	83	32 5/8	122	48
6	2 3/8	45	17 3/4	84	33	123	48 3/8
7	2 1/4	46	18 1/8	85	33 1/2	124	48 7/8
8	3 1/8	47	18 1/2	86	33 7/8	125	49 1/4
9	3 1/2	48	18 7/8	87	34 1/4	126	49 5/8
10	4	49	19 1/4	88	34 5/8	127	50
11	4 3/8	50	19 5/8	89	35	128	50 3/8
12	4 3/4	51	20	90	35 1/2	129	50 3/4
13	5 1/8	52	20 1/2	91	35 7/8	130	51 1/8
14	5 1/2	53	20 7/8	92	36 1/4	131	51 5/8
15	5 7/8	54	21 1/4	93	36 5/8	132	52
16	6 1/4	55	21 5/8	94	37	133	52 3/8
17	6 3/4	56	22	95	37 3/8	134	52 3/4
18	7 1/8	57	22 1/2	96	37 3/4	135	53 1/8
19	7 1/2	58	22 7/8	97	38 1/4	136	53 1/2
20	7 7/8	59	23 1/4	98	38 5/8	137	53 7/8
21	8 1/4	60	23 5/8	99	39	138	54 3/8
22	8 5/8	61	24	100	39 3/8	139	54 3/4
23	9	62	24 3/8	101	39 3/4	140	55 1/8
24	9 1/2	63	24 3/4	102	40 1/8	141	55 1/2
25	9 7/8	64	25 1/4	103	40 1/2	142	55 7/8
26	10 1/4	65	25 5/8	104	41	143	56 1/2
27	10 5/8	66	26	105	41 3/8	144	56 3/4
28	11	67	26 3/8	106	41 3/4	145	57
29	11 3/8	68	26 3/4	107	42 1/8	146	57 1/2
30	11 7/8	69	27 1/8	108	42 1/2	147	57 7/8
31	12 1/4	70	27 1/2	109	42 7/8	148	58 1/4
32	12 5/8	71	28	110	43 1/4	149	58 5/8
33	13	72	28 3/8	111	43 3/4	150	59
34	13 3/8	73	28 3/4	112	44 1/8	151	59 1/2
35	13 3/4	74	29 1/8	113	44 1/2	152	59 7/8
36	14 1/8	75	29 1/2	114	44 7/8	153	60 1/4
37	14 5/8	76	29 7/8	115	45 1/4		
38	15	77	30 1/4	116	45 5/8		
39	15 3/8	78	30 3/4	117	46		

Special Skills

CABLES

Cables are twists in the knitting where the stitches appear braided. To make a cable, you place the first half of the stitches in the cable pattern on a separate cable needle, knit the second half, then knit the stitches on the cable needle. This twists the stitches. The pattern will tell you how many stitches and whether to hold them to the front (for a left cable) or the back (for a right cable). See Abbreviations (page 131) for specific instructions.

Left Cable

1. Slip the next few stitches onto the cable needle (the pattern will tell you how many; here it's 3) and hold the cable needle in front of the work.

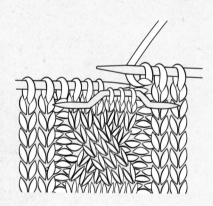

2. Knit next few stitches from left needle (again, the pattern will tell you how many; here it's 3).

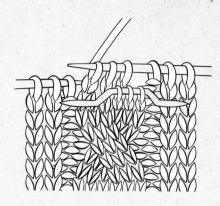

3. Knit the stitches from the cable needle.

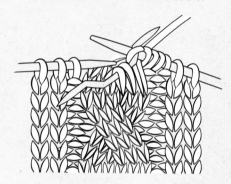

STRANDED KNITTING

When you knit with two colors at the same time, you keep the yarn not in use along the back of the knitting. (For the Tourniquet Scarf [page 36], you carry both colors together and move them back and forth together as you're knitting and changing colors.)

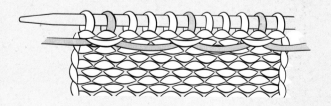

Keep the yarn that runs on the back fairly loose. If the stranded yarn is pulled too tight it will make the fabric pucker and distort.

As you knit, wrap the yarn not being used around the working yarn every few stitches to secure it.

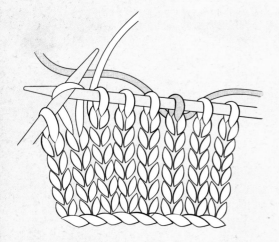

DUPLICATE STITCH
This stitch is worked on top of a knit stitch after the knitting is completed.

Thread a yarn needle with the desired yarn. Bring the needle from back to front below the stitch you want to cover. Bring the thread over the right-hand leg of the stitch, going down into the fabric at the top of the stitch and coming up again at the bottom. Trace over the lefthand leg the same way. Repeat where you want the next stitch to be.

3-NEEDLE BIND-OFF
This technique binds off two pieces, creating a seam between them. It is great for the shoulder seams of sweaters.

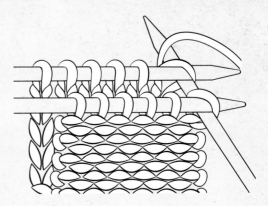

Hold the two knit pieces with right sides facing (unless directed otherwise). With a third needle, knit into the first stitch on each needle, knitting these two stitches together. Repeat with the second stitch on both needles, then pull the first stitch over the second. Continue across the row until all stitches are bound off.

SHORT ROWS
Short rows are used to shape a garment. The method used to do this is called Wrap & Turn.

Short Rows with Wrapped Stitches
This technique is used to insert extra rows invisibly in the middle of the knitting to create soft curves or extra fullness in the fabric (see the Corset on page 63). They are rows that are only partially worked before turning. You wrap the next stitch before turning a short row to avoid creating holes where you turned the work. When working the row following a wrapped stitch, you hide the wrap by picking it up along with the stitch.

Wrap and Turn (W & T)

1. Knit to the specified stitch, then slip this stitch onto the right needle, bring the yarn from back to front, "wrapping" the stitch.

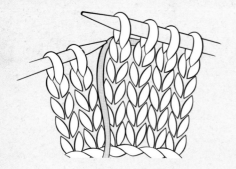

2. Slip the same stitch back to the left needle.

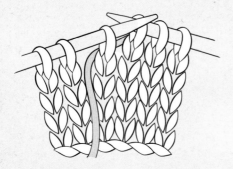

3. Turn the work; bring the yarn to the front or back (depending on whether you are knitting or purling), to complete the wrap. Finish working the row.

UW (unwrap stitch): Knitting

Insert the needle under the wrap from bottom to top, front to back, then knitwise into the stitch itself. Knit the wrap and the stitch together. When stitches have two wraps, work them both together with the stitch.

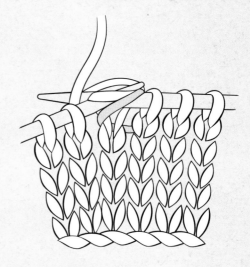

UW (unwrap stitch): Purling

Insert the needle into the wrap from bottom to top, back to front, then purlwise into the stitch itself. Purl the wrap and the stitch together.

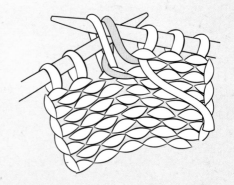

I-CORD

Use double-pointed needles to create a narrow tube used for making ties or button loops.

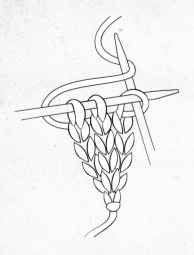

Cast on 3 stitches (or the number specified in the instructions). Knit one row. Keeping the double-pointed needle in the same hand and without turning it, slide the stitches to the other end of the needle and knit them again, pulling the working yarn tight across the back as you knit the first stitch. Continue knitting like this, gently pulling on the cord as it is being formed, until the I-cord is as long as the pattern specifies.

KITCHENER STITCH

Kitchener Stitch is a method of grafting to sets of live stitches together without leaving a seam. These instructions are for grafting stockinette.

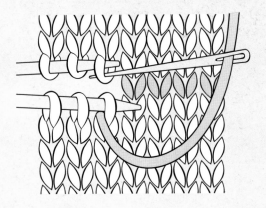

Thread a tail 3 to 4 times the length of the edge being grafted onto a tapestry needle. Hold the needles with an equal number of live stitches parallel to each other with the tips pointing in the same direction and the right (knit) sides facing up. Insert the tapestry needle purlwise into the first stitch on the front knitting needle, draw the yarn through, but do not drop the stitch from the needle. Insert the tapestry needle knitwise into the first stitch on the back knitting needle. Draw the yarn through. Do not drop the stitch from the knitting needle. *Insert the tapestry needle knitwise into the first stitch on the front needle, drop the stitch from the needle. Insert the tapestry needle purlwise into the next stitch on the front needle. Draw the yarn through. Do not drop the stitch from the knitting needle. Insert the needle purlwise into first stitch on the back needle. Drop the stitch from knitting needle. Insert the tapestry needle knitwise into the next stitch on the back needle. Draw yarn through but do not drop stitch from knitting needle.* Repeat from * to * until all live stitches have been grafted.

About the Author

Genevieve Miller is a southern California native who learned how to knit when she was 11. After reading TWILIGHT by Stephenie Meyer, she was inspired to design her own knits. She's happily married to a great guy who doesn't mind the house being taken over by a giant yarn stash and the mother of three kids who are willing to wear things knitted by mom. After teaching kindergarten, fourth grade, and the dramatic arts for eight years, Genevieve took time off to be a stay-at-home mom. She lives in Pasadena, CA, where she can be found reading vampire fiction, knitting, or teaching kids how to knit. For VAMPIRE KNITS she designed the Tourniquet Scarf and the Imprint Pillow.

Contributing Designers

Toni Carr (LOVE BITES–FOR HIM) is a roller girl, designer, and coffee shop owner. She is the author of *Knockdown Knits*. She can be found online at joanofdark.com.

Teri Christensen (PAW WARMERS) learned to knit from her cute Danish neighbor in 2004, and since then it's become a serious addiction. Her knit designs have been published on The Leaky Cauldron, in Debbie Stoller's 2008 Stitch 'n Bitch Page-a-Day Calendar, in Famazon Magazine's *Twilight*-themed issue, on Ravelry and on her blog at stitchnsnitch.wordpress.com. She lives in Salt Lake City, UT.

Sara Delaney (SHAPESHIFTER SHRUG) was taught to crochet and knit at an early age by her mémère. Sara is currently a teacher in residence at WEBS: America's Yarn Store in Northampton, MA. Her musings and projects can be found at her blog, ChickenBetty. wordpress.com.

Kimberly Dijkstra (RAMPAGE FISHNET GLOVES, BLOODY SOCKS, THE BLACK VEIL, GLAMOUR EARRINGS AND SANGRIA BRACELET) is a 22-year-old knitter and crocheter from East Meadow, NY. She enjoys incorporating beads and embroidery into her work and using materials that provide an interesting texture.

Ashley Fay (SITIO STOCKINGS, BE STILL MY BEATING HEART CAPELET, SIDHE LACE SHRUG, "TEAM EDWARD" and "TEAM JACOB" CHARTS for VAMPIRE TOTES) is 21 years old. She is a dancer, fashion designer, knitter, and scholar extraordinaire. She lives in Yucaipa, CA.

Nancy Fry (PALM READERS) lives in Connecticut with her husband and their two wonderful kids. She taught herself to knit about seven years ago has been addicted to knitting ever since.

Bethe Galantino (BELLISSIMA MITTENS) is the owner of a small gift shop in central Massachusetts and is hopelessly addicted to knitting. She spins, crochets, and sews too.

Tanis Gray (SILVER BULLET-AND-BLOOD HEAD SCARF, "GOT BLOOD?" PILLOW, and BLOOD BOTTLE COZIES) is an honors graduate of RISD and a resident of Washington, DC. She has published more than 150 knitting designs, and has served as yarn editor at *Vogue Knitting* and as coeditor of *knit.1* magazine.

Abigail Horsfall (WEREWOLF HAT) lives in the Seattle, WA, area with her husband and two cats. She has been knitting for many years and began designing when she couldn't find the right hat pattern.

Nikol Lohr (THE PRIM REAPER'S CORSET) is the creator of Yarn School and the author of *Naughty Needles: Sexy, Saucy Knits for the Bedroom and Beyond*. She blogs at The Thrifty Knitter (thriftyknitter.com) and is cupcake on Ravelry and queenievonsugarpants on Flickr.

Marilee Norris (DESCENT INTO DARKNESS WRAP, VAMPIRE TOTES including "BE SAFE" CHART and ALPHABET CHARTS) taught herself how to knit at the age of 27 and has not stopped since. You can find her on ravelry.com as Mariblue, and visit her blog at bloglessknitting.blogspot.com. She lives in the Pacific Northwest.

Kathie Pendry (PULSE PROTECTORS) is a high school history teacher on hiatus while she raises her two young daughters. She and her family are currently living in South Korea on a government contract.

Rilana Riley-Munson (COUNTESS BATHORY SCARF) resides in Portland, OR, with her husband, two daughters, and three cats. Her Vintage Girl Cloche was published in Debbie Stoller's 2008 Stitch 'n Bitch Page-a-Day Calendar.

Cirilia Rose (LORE HOODIE) knits and designs in the Northeast and is inspired by all things cinematic. Her favorite vampire is the wickedly funny Spike from Joss Whedon's *Buffy the Vampire Slayer*.

Stephanie Spiers (VAMPIRE DIARY PROTECTOR) recently moved from Sarnia, Ontario, Canada, to the UK. She picked up knitting in college and has been steadily knitting over the past four years.

Julie Turjoman (UNDER COVER OF MIDNIGHT HOODED COWL) knits, designs, and writes in northern California. She is the author of *Brave New Knits: Dozens of Projects and Personalities From the Knitting Blogosphere*. In addition, her patterns have been published in *Interweave Knits* and *Twist Collective*. Find out more on her website, julieturjoman.com.

Tonya Wagner (LITTLE FANG SWEATER) has contributed designs to *Interweave Knits*, the UK publication *Yarn Forward*, and the book *Knitting in the Sun*. Tonya lives in Louisville, KY, with her husband and two children. Her website is theshizknit.com.

INDEX